How I Made
FORTUNES in REAL ESTATE
and How You Can Too!

BARBARA KNAUF

How I Made FORTUNES in REAL ESTATE *and How You Can Too!*

Fascinating Stories and Secrets for Success from an Insider

ARCHWAY PUBLISHING

Archway Publishing books may be ordered through booksellers or by contacting:

Archway Publishing
1663 Liberty Drive
Bloomington, IN 47403
www.archwaypublishing.com
1-(888)-242-5904

The information, ideas, and suggestions in this book are not intended to
render professional advice. Before following any suggestions contained
in this book, you should consult your personal accountant or other
financial advisor. Neither the author nor the publisher shall be liable or
responsible for any loss or damage allegedly arising as a consequence of
your use or application of any information or suggestions in this book.

Because of the dynamic nature of the Internet, any web addresses or
links contained in this book may have changed since publication and
may no longer be valid. The views expressed in this work are solely those
of the author and do not necessarily reflect the views of the publisher,
and the publisher hereby disclaims any responsibility for them.

ISBN: 978-1-4808-1343-4 (sc)
ISBN: 978-1-4808-1342-7 (hc)
ISBN: 978-1-4808-1344-1 (e)

Library of Congress Control Number: 2014921895

Printed in the United States of America.

Archway Publishing rev. date: 3/18/2015

"You have to learn the rules of the game. And then you have to play better than anyone else."

—Albert Einstein

Someone once asked Albert Einstein how he was able to achieve so much in his lifetime. He supposedly said that he did everything at once, did not put anything off until later. Those words have been an inspiration to me all my life. I also believe that everyone should strive to be the best they can be in anything they do. Not so much for financial gain, as that comes automatically with doing things right, but for self-respect and the joy of achievement. I also always tried to leave each place I owned in my life better than I found it.

CONTENTS

Chapter 5

Chapter 6

Chapter 7

Chapter 8

INTRODUCTION

The only true fortunes I ever made in
my life were in real estate.

After nearly twenty years in real estate as a sales agent and mortgage broker in California and as an agent on the other side of this continent, in Florida, I believe I have earned the right to speak about real estate—to tell a few interesting stories and to shed some more light on the forces that bring changes in the real estate world that affect the entire economy in a large way. I have sold properties and brokered loans for more than $100 million, working as an independent, associate sale and loan agent in California, as well as a real estate agent in Florida.

I have been a Realtor with various companies on both sides of the country. I have made many hundreds of thousands of dollars in real estate, and I have bought and sold many properties for myself as well. I have purchased "fixers" for about $400,000 and sold them for more than a million in a span of two years several times. I have bought homes here in Kansas City, where this book is written, and in Florida and California. I have listed and sold homes ranging from $52,000 to $4.5 million and every price in between.

I lived in million-dollar homes for more than thirty years and just recently downsized to a smaller home in Kansas City after a move here to be close to my younger daughter. I drove Mercedes, Lexus, and Jaguar cars while working in real estate for years. I bought art and antiques and vacationed in Europe, the Bahamas and Mexico all the time. My lifestyle drastically improved as a real estate agent/investor beyond anything I had experienced before as an entrepreneur. And that life allowed me to come home from work every night!

And if I could do all these things as an immigrant from Germany with just a baccalaureate, so can you! But you need to make that decision and dedicate yourself to the process.

I may not have become a billionaire, which seems to be the number now that impresses people in this time of superlatives. But if you are thinking about leaving a nine-to-five job, making your own schedule, and creating wealth and real estate holdings for security, then this book is for you. You can benefit from my knowledge and also from my mistakes, which I will share here as well so that you can avoid them. And perhaps you will be so successful that you become a billionaire! It is up to you to make it happen.

CHAPTER 1

I came to the United States from Germany ...

I came to the United States from Germany as a twenty-one-year-old woman with $300, a suitcase, and a job as a Pan American Airlines stewardess. By all standards I was poor, but I had a great job despite the low pay. I flew around the globe for more than six years and had a fabulous time. For many years I was a renter without any significant savings or assets, and I was just making a living in other careers. But when I became a licensed real estate agent, it all changed. I now own houses in Florida, Kansas City, and California. I sold and financed tens of millions of dollars of real estate, and in the process I also made money for my many clients with my advice to them. It is all about making the right choices in real estate. Here in this book is what I have learned and the mistakes I have made. I hope that you will profit from all of it. But first is a glimpse into my life and my story and how I became a real estate investor.

After marrying and having to leave Pan Am because of their old-fashioned rules at the time—that you could not be married and continue to fly—I tried my luck with bringing American ice cream to Germany after a divorce from the pilot I had married. I obtained the franchise rights to Baskin-Robbins for Germany at no cost, based on my knowledge of Germany. I opened two stores, one in Cologne and the other in Düsseldorf. The ice cream franchises necessitated my leaving the United States and taking my two young daughters to Germany, which meant a complete change of life. The stores were successful; it was the first time German people had more than the four flavors they were used to. They now had thirty-one flavors! However, operating the stores in Germany was not easy. The food laws were much stricter; no artificial flavors or colors were allowed, and the ice cream had to be imported from Belgium. Every week the German health inspectors took samples of the ice cream to check the bacteria count. (When ice cream melts, the bacteria count increases dramatically.) I had to destroy much ice cream. I also had to spend a lot of time on freeways commuting from town to town. The Italian Mafia controlled all ice cream parlors in Germany at that time, something I had not known before I arrived there. I was threatened twice, and my daughters wanted to return to the United States. When we did return after selling the stores for a nice profit, I had to come up with a new way to make a living. I began by working for an importer in Connecticut to learn the import business.

We settled again in Connecticut, where we had come from. I started my new business a year later and imported a line of gift items I had designed. They were big hits at gift trade shows. I sold to Hallmark stores nationwide and thousands of smaller gift stores. Importing my products from Asia required a lot of expensive travel (to Korea in particular), staying in hotels, and investing large amounts of funds into merchandise I had yet to sell. Again my daughters were left with housekeepers for days at a time, something I disliked doing and always worried about.

After six successful years I was blown out of business by a much larger competitor who undersold my products and actually stole my copyrights and trademarks. This led to an eight-year lawsuit, which left me with a settlement; however, the attorneys took the largest part of this settlement.

Once again I had to find a new way to make a living. I met some friends who were successful in real estate in California at that time, and I decided to get into real estate. There was a light at the end of the tunnel. Copyright infringement is not possible in real estate. I could return to my home every night. It was perfect.

The proceeds from the import lawsuit settlement bought my first house in California. I purchased it for $325,000 and sold it for $575,000 just two years later. I had made only some marginal changes to the house. I took down ghastly wallpaper, painted the walls, and did some minor landscaping. However, I did decorate the house very nicely with my furnishings and artwork. It looked great. Taking a profit of $250,000 in two years was a lot easier than working every day with travel expenses, standing at trade shows all over the country for ten hours per day, and leaving my daughters in the care of housekeepers while I was absent.

To illustrate many important rules in real estate, I will be telling you several entertaining stories. They were chosen out of hundreds I could write about to highlight certain points you need to know. These stories are all based on facts and events that really occurred. There are many happy stories as well, but they were more routine and do not help to explain possible pitfalls. You need to learn which problem areas you need to avoid.

Though I also have much experience as a mortgage broker, this book concentrates on residential real estate. Commercial real estate is in a different category, and loans are a completely different subject that needs to be addressed separately. Though all real estate dealings and financing go hand in hand, of course.

This writing does not cover textbook matters you learn about in real estate school. It deals with all the other everyday matters you need to know to make the right choices in real estate, whether you are an agent, an investor, buyer or seller. If you follow my guidelines and learn from my experiences, you will be another success story!

For success in real estate as a career ...

For success in real estate as a career, you have to follow several ground rules. These rules in this industry never change, despite electronic changes, new computer programs, changing markets and mortgage rates, company mergers, and so on.

Your age does not matter; you can start at a young age or later in life. I began my real estate career at age forty-two! It was going to be the third business career of my life.

These are some basic truths for success in real estate

1. You need to be willing to work long hours.
2. You need to focus on your goal and let nothing stand in your way or sidetrack you.
3. You need to make a plan for yourself as to where you want to be five years from the day you start on your new career.
4. Setting a goal is an important psychological part of success.
5. Project confidence, never seem unsure, and remember that your clients will, in all probability, know less than you do.

© Lynette Yencho

6. If you don't know the answer to a question you are asked, just tell your client that you will research it, or consult with your broker or another agent right away for the answer. Don't say that you don't know.
7. Dress for success. You have heard that before, and it is most important!
8. Be well groomed. Agents with unkempt appearances, dirty fingernails, and food in their beards will quickly lose clients to someone else.
9. Stay in contact with your clients while you are having a transaction with them. Call them often, and do not keep a mysterious silence. They will think you have no interest in their deal. Keep them up-to-date at all times.
10. Always conduct yourself with integrity and honesty.
11. Treat all clients with respect no matter what they look like and who they are.
12. You need to market yourself; this is very important.
13. Keep your personal life private; a client is not your friend.
14. Send a thank-you note or bring a gift to your client after the transaction is closed.
15. Always stay in touch with your past clients. Send cards; call from time to time for follow-ups. They may have a family member or friend who may need an efficient real estate agent.

A story to learn from

The following is a story to learn from (see item 11 above):

I had a listing for $2.4 million, and it was a new listing for me. On the first open house no one came to see it but some neighbors. On the second open house a young man in shorts and flip-flops drove up with a young woman and some children. They were all very casually dressed, and the car was nondescript. They had been driving around in the neighborhood. I thought that they could never afford this house, but I courteously showed them around. Soon the kids were screaming, "We love it! We love it"!

The woman smiled, and the young man pulled out his checkbook and wrote a deposit check on the spot for $20,000. He had made a fortune in the software industry and bought the house for cash for his girlfriend and her children. He did not bargain, either.

I deposited the check with my company and mailed the contracts to him. The deal closed without a hitch. He was one of the first viewers of the property and had made many millions to play with. And I made a double commission.

Moral of the story: It's the old cliché: Never judge a book by its cover!

©Lynette Yencho

Your real estate license

Getting your real estate license is the first step to success, of course.

You can log on to the Internet and Google for "real estate licenses" in your state or town. The various schools and companies that are licensed by the state to give classes will appear.

Obviously you want to find the one that is closest to your home or take an online course, which is also available. You need to learn the basics of real estate. In Florida I chose an interactive real estate school with a physical teacher over an online program. The subject matter can be pretty dry at times, and I had heard that a particular teacher at a real estate school in south Florida was very funny. And I laughed all the way through the course! The instructor made it fun and entertaining. I enjoyed my evening classes very much.

After completing your first course in real estate principles and practices and other elective or mandatory courses, you will know the mechanics and basics of real estate. You will learn about the code of ethics in real estate, fair housing laws, surveying basics, real estate math, real estate law, zoning, appraisals, and more.

At the end of the course in your particular state, you will take a test. It is given by the school and is preparatory for the test given by the state to obtain your license. There are no limits to how often you can take the state examination. I have heard of people who took it twelve times until they passed, but most pass it on the first try.

Your instructor will let you know where to go for the state examination; he or she will send your "certificate of completion" to the state. A word of advice here: you have to apply for the state exam yourself immediately after you pass your first test. Since there are hundreds of applicants all the time, it may take three to four weeks to get an appointment for the state license exam. The sooner you take that one-hundred-question exam, the better, as many of the things you learned will still be fresh in your mind. You will take this state exam on a computer in a facility provided by the state.

Your test is immediately checked for correctness, so you will know right away if you passed or not! When I passed, I was overjoyed! The courses and tests were behind me now, and I was on the road to success—as you will be!

You can always take more elective courses in every state to broaden your knowledge. The Division of Real Estate of the State of Florida, for example, offers various online courses about statutes and rules and licensing requirements. Once you obtain your initial license to do business, you need to renew it after eighteen months, and after that every two years. The renewals can be made on the Internet with a small fee. Google is a fantastic resource to search for licensing requirements in your state. They do vary from state to state, so do your research to get to your end goal!

Now you have your license and you know the basics, but you will not know about the everyday real events that will take place while you are working in this exciting business. There is a large difference between theory and practice, and no one can teach you that in a classroom. You have to get out there and go for it!

For some people, an easier way into the business is to work as an assistant to another top agent in a successful real estate company for some time to get your feet wet. Starting out as an assistant with a pro in the field might be an invaluable experience and could be a lot of fun, as well. You will learn along the way and get paid a salary to cover your living expenses.

Learn from this mistake

When I first applied for my Florida license after leaving California where my license was still valid, I thought it would be a breeze to pass the test. After all, I had lots of experience. But it was not easy. The rules are different in every state of the Union, although they are very similar overall. I had to learn the Florida facts. At first I did not study very hard at all and thought I could just sail through the state examination. I failed the first time by two errors I had made. There are a total of one hundred questions, which you need to complete within a specific time frame. This failure caused me to open the books online and sit down to pass the exam again quickly, as the longer one is away from the subject matter, the easier it is to forget the many small details the exam asks for. There are many variations of the exam; the second test was different from the first one I took.

The person giving the Florida real estate course I had attended gave us some of the questions on his test to prepare us for the state test. Previously, I had experienced some less than satisfactory dealings with other agents while purchasing my investment properties in Florida. I thought at the time the agents in Florida were not up to par and seemingly not as well informed as the agents I knew in California. Somehow they must have finagled their way through the state exam, I thought. But the examination proved to be much more difficult. The second time around I passed, to my great relief.

So study the books; there is no shortcut here! If I could do it, so can you!

Real estate personality

If you are timid and cannot make decisions easily, are not a self-starter, or like to be told what to do, this industry may not be for you; however, some people are late bloomers! If you have lots of energy, like sales and people in general, like to explore, and have a certain amount of creativity, a basic knowledge of math, and, most importantly, the drive to succeed, real estate is the path to a successful and rewarding career and life.

As with any other sales job, it further helps if you know how to smile, have no prejudices, and have a positive manner. People tend to stay away from sullen, negative human beings, and that holds true in real estate, as well. Perhaps you have come across a morose, depressing Realtor. It is not enjoyable to go scouting for your dream property with such a person. It will leave you feeling let down, rather than filled with excitement. This type is usually someone who makes negative remarks about everything, rather than pointing out the positive features of a property you might be looking at. Stay away from a person like that whether you are selling or buying.

Marketing yourself

So now you have your license and are hanging your hat in an office you feel comfortable with. What now? Fortunately there are many ways to market yourself and create business. Please note that I said "create"! None of this is taught in real estate schools. But the advice I give you here is proven; it works!

1. If you own a home, place it on the market, even if you don't really want to move. You will have your first listing, perhaps even get a price you did not dream of and decide to sell after all. You can advertise it, have open houses, and place it on the MLS (Multiple Listing Service) in your area. You will get calls from potential buyers. If they don't like your house, you can suggest another one or several more and show them those other homes. You will have some leads now.

2. "Farming an area." Choose a nice area not too far from your office or home, and send out postcards to all the owners with interesting information—that is, a home that just sold or one that was just listed. It does not have to be your own house. It can be anybody's. But you may want

to add that you were not the "procuring" agent, or you may get an angry call from the agent who actually made the deal. People still open their mail every day, even in this time of electronic communications. I found that snail mail works wonderfully. You will get calls.

3. "Social media marketing." Obviously you want to do Facebook, LinkedIn, Twitter, etc., and let people know you are now a real estate agent and could help them with their searches and purchases or sales.

4. Create your own website to highlight your special skills, i.e. dedication to your clients, other language skills, knowledge of the market, sales successes, advertising your own listings and the listings of your office and more. Let your imagination fly high!

5. Old-fashioned door knocking. This means you walk from house to house in a neighborhood and inquire if the residents might know someone interested in your services.

6. Cold-calling. I knew a successful agent who spent much time calling people listed in a Marin County phone book to ask if they were thinking about selling. He made at least $100,000 each year with that method and had many referrals. He never spent a dime on advertising.

7. Business cards. Have business cards printed right away, and hand them out to every single person you meet. On the back of the card imprint that you appreciate referrals. Often people don't think about that and are happy to refer people they know to you if you ask. Word of mouth is a great source of business.

8. Advertising in magazines that are local and are read by many. An ad does not have to be large, and it should always include your photo.

9. Buy For Sale signs with your photo on them for your listings, and place them in front of your listings where they can easily be seen.

10. Ask your company to promote you; perhaps they have a plan. Ask them to advertise the fact that you joined the company. If you don't ask, you probably don't get.

11. Be socially active, and hand out your cards. I know a friend who received a call from a person he had met on a golf course a year earlier, and he now sold him a house. This person had saved his business card for a year!

12. E-mail all your friends and relatives telling them that you are now the proud owner of a real estate license and have become part of a successful agency. Do not be shy about it!

13. Join the National Association of Realtors and become a Realtor; it is more impressive! But there is a fee for it.

14. Do whatever you can think of yourself! Again, be creative!

Real estate company brokers

As an agent you will always work under a broker in any office anywhere. The broker shoulders all responsibilities for an office's transactions and ongoing business. Some companies are owned by large corporations, and the broker is employed by the corporation. Some brokers own their own offices. In some states like Florida, the broker is also the mediator, arbitrator, and final decision maker in disputes and negotiations. This is important to know, since as an agent you will have a right to legal counsel, but the broker will make all decisions that will affect your transactions and your status as an agent with the company.

Brokers come in many shapes, sizes, nationalities, and abilities—just like agents. Some have a sense of humor, some never twitch a muscle in their face, some speak other languages as well, some are tall, and some are short. Some will treat you with respect; some will abuse their power. When you go to an interview with a broker, make sure you like that person. If you sense there might be a compatibility problem, don't work for that person or company. It's basic good sense. Most brokers are educated and knowledgeable, and want to have you on their team. Some companies will not hire new agents; others do. Most brokers/companies want as many agents as possible. Some have dozens of agents working in their offices or out of their homes.

You can always ask your broker for advice, a

comforting possibility for the inexperienced or novice agent. Brokers can hire and fire at any time. It is a good idea to be on a good footing with the broker in your office.

The broker can and will scrutinize your files and have open access to them at any time. He or she is responsible, after all, for your actions. Each purchase contract you write or lease you complete for a client as an agent will be submitted to the broker for final approval. This is a much-needed rule, as otherwise agents could commit major transgressions without intending to do so, simply because they are inexperienced or make a mistake. The broker needs to have a broker's license with the state he or she lives in. This state examination is much more stringent and complicated than an agent's license examination. The broker's license needs to be renewed periodically, just like an agent's license. These renewals can be made electronically through the Internet by going online to your state's department of state, real estate licensing division.

Some agents are brokers as well but prefer to work for another broker and company rather than their own.

Your real estate associates

The betrayal story

Be cautious with your Realtor friends; learn from my mistakes. A colleague of mine in California worked for the same company I was working with. I had not yet learned the rule to never to introduce another Realtor to possible clients. It's a very bad mistake. My old-time possible clients/friends were from Europe originally. They lived in a lovely house in the county and owned a beautiful, large yacht, which they kept in a nearby harbor. I had gone out sailing with them many times, and I always enjoyed these days very much. Their home was beautifully tucked into the California hills and had been added to and enlarged. This home was now worth well over a million dollars.

In good faith I naively introduced my real estate woman friend to my friendly couple. She now came along on the yacht outings and also to the home of the Europeans. Are you seeing the end of the story? Well, of course, this is how it developed.

One day I received a phone call from her. She informed me out of the blue that my friends had listed their home with her for over a million dollars, and that she had found another house for them for just under one million. She said that she wanted to be the one I would hear the news from and not "from a stranger"! Actually, I would have preferred hearing the news from a stranger rather than from my so-called friend. An honorable real estate person would have suggested what is called a "co-listing," when both agents work with the clients and then share the rewards. After all, I had made the introduction, and I had a much better sales record than this woman ever had. She had not sold a house in years!

Realtors are always competing and sometimes will do whatever it takes to get to the top. The companies they work for will reward them with plaques and framed certificates for their work and actually purposely foster the atmosphere of competition. There are many ruthless people in the business. It turned out my best friend was one of those and stepped right on me and over me. So be careful and keep your friends to yourself ... sad, but true. And you won't have such a disappointment.

My former friend made a lot of money in both transactions. A lesson learned? Well, yes! Had I wanted to learn it? No! It was painful! It wasn't so much the loss of income (I could afford that), but it was the betrayal that hurt!

Working as a real estate agent

Real estate has always been the second largest economic driving factor in the country, after Wall Street and the "building industry," or construction. Of course construction and real estate go hand in hand. One cannot exist without the other. It takes Realtors to sell most homes, however, salespeople for new development construction are usually employed by the "builders" and do not need to have a real estate license; hence they can tell you a good story—just about anything to make a sale—as there really is no overseeing institution.

Realtors sell all the other properties, unless they are "for sale by owner," whether residential or commercial. Some are brokers; some are real estate sales agents. Brokers can work for themselves and by themselves; an agent works with a real estate company as an independent contractor. They do not receive salaries or bonuses; they work strictly for commissions and pay their own costs connected with their work and their own taxes. Most real estate companies will provide desks for free to agents. Some charge a monthly fee for the desk and charge for every paper copy they make in the office; however, there are other advantages to working for such a real estate company.

Some offices provide computers to work with. Most agents will have their own laptops, iPads, and iPhones, where they store all their information. Most pay for advertising their listings, insurance, car expenses, and living expenses. They have to pay small fees for being linked into the Multiple Listing Service to list their properties for sale; they have to pay for the lockboxes they use and the keys to access the boxes. Agents need to pay for their license, their school to get the license, and fees to the state and Board of Realtors to keep the license. They must also be a member of the National Board of Realtors to keep the license. In addition, they have to pay a yearly fee for errors and omissions insurance, as no company will hire them without this insurance paid for up front. These are expenses agents need to expect. (However, don't hold your breath if you expect to get a dollar out of the insurance!)

Here is a word of advice: If you cannot afford all these costs and don't have enough money saved to cover living expenses for a while without making a larger commission, you may fail. If you prepare yourself and know what to expect after reading this book, you will succeed. Perhaps you can keep a part-time job or have a partner who will support you during the first few months, and you will be on the road to success.

Without some savings or someone who will support you at first, or without the will to succeed, you may not make it in this extremely competitive business. So prepare yourself and expect to have to learn while having fun, as this is a people's business and dealing with people and real estate is a lot of fun!

It took years of working and many mistakes on my part to learn what I am telling you in this book. So go ahead and venture out! After reading my book you will be way ahead of many others. There's no more need to buy many books on different real estate matters or to read hundreds of articles in different publications. The information you need to be successful is right here in a nutshell!

Real estate agent safety advice

Here is some advice all agents should follow while working in this profession. We all wish for the perfect working conditions, but sadly we also have to deal with the realities of life today … which may include unpleasant situations. Though such situations are very rare, it is best to be prepared; therefore, I am including the following list of safety measures to observe.

From time to time agents become the target for criminals while showing houses. This is unfortunate, but it has happened all over the country. It is therefore very important to follow safety guidelines at all times for your protection and well-being.

1. Obtain the name, address, and phone numbers of your clients before showing properties. Verify their IDs, and don't be shy about it. You have a right to know who your clients are and who will take up your time.
2. It is best to meet new clients at your office first before setting off to show houses.
3. Never meet a stranger at a listing for a showing.
4. Always take your cell phone with you, and have it in your hand while doing showings, so you can dial 911 if you need to.
5. Carry a pepper spray with you in your purse or pocket within easy reach.
6. Leave front doors wide open whenever showing any vacant house or if the owners have left for the showing, even in winter. Showings take a short time.
7. Do not walk into remote areas of a house with your new client if it is a large home with several floors, without another person present. Usually, if you show a property to a family or a couple, there is nothing to worry about.
8. Let your office know which properties you are showing. Keep your office informed about your whereabouts.
9. When holding open houses, have visitors sign your guest list and ask for phone numbers. If visitors don't want to give that information, politely ask them to leave. Explain that the owners wish to know who came into their home.
10. Try to have someone else with you at open houses if you are in a remote area or it is a vacant property; it could be your husband, wife, or a friend.

11. Should you feel threatened or uneasy about a person, follow your instincts and stay by the front door or leave.
12. Use common sense, and place your safety first over trying to sell a house.

Agent commissions

Usually you start at the 50 percent level (50 percent of the overall commission is paid to you and the other 50 percent to the broker) for services when you bring no experience with you, and only your enthusiasm and personality. Commissions are staggered according to properties sold and the money flow they generate. Some offices pay differently from others, and some offices may negotiate your commission structure. It pays to investigate their commission policies, and don't be shy about it. Ask and be clear about it. Try to negotiate the best commission percentage you can get, and always ask how soon they pay after a deal closes. Get this information in writing. It will be important for your personal life. You don't want to wait for months to get paid.

The highest commissions paid are at 85 percent of the commissions charged to the sellers. Usually sellers pay all commissions unless payment is otherwise negotiated. Sometimes a buyer may pay the agent's commission—if the seller objects to paying it or if the buyer wants an exclusive agent relationship with the agent he or she is working with and is willing to pay the commission. I have never seen it, but it is possible.

During my most productive years in real estate as an agent, I made 85 percent commissions, which put me in the highest, or one percent income bracket, of all agents in the country. From 50 percent commissions you go to 55 percent, to 60 percent, to 70 percent, and so on. Some companies will start a new agent at a 55 percent commission; try to negotiate that!

See the following commission example:

The sales price of a property is	$250,000
The seller pays 5 percent commissions overall, or	$12,500
Listing broker/agent gets 2.5 percent, or	$6,250
Selling broker/buyer's agent gets 2.5 percent, or	$6,250
At a 50 percent split between broker and agent, the agents will each receive	$3,125

Now figure out your commission at a 60 percent split between your broker and yourself instead of the 50 percent split. If you cannot do that even with a calculator, you might be better off with a different line of work. But as I said before, if I can do it, so can you!

Easily raking in commissions?

No, not really. I can truthfully say that each of my commissions was truthfully and honestly earned.

And it was well worth it. I often worked seven days a week, sometimes ten hours a day. Clients will call you at all hours; my pager then and my cell phone more recently were always going. They would call early in the mornings, on holidays, late at night, and on weekends. Of course on Sundays we had to have open houses. If you have several listings, which every good agent has, you have to alternate Sundays to accommodate all your sellers. Or your assistant will help out with that. To get away, I sometimes left the country and was not reachable at all—and everything usually was just fine upon my return as I always notified my clients about my vacations.

I loved what I was doing, and I gave my business all my attention. My children were grown and away at college. I had the time, and I enjoyed being successful.

I met many lovely people, and doing transactions with them was a pleasure. It worked well both ways. When you are dealing with high-priced homes as I was and your clients are reasonable and intelligent, it is often easier to sell such homes than the lower-priced ones. In transactions with lower-priced homes, the seller and buyer tend to cling to every penny as if their life depended on it, or they are unreasonable about the value of their property. I called it having "unrealistic expectations" about their houses. Then it takes a lot of work and showings of similar-priced properties to get down to the true value with either the buyer or the seller.

But whatever type of property or value you are dealing with, no sale or commission has ever been made overnight. But do you know of many other legitimate businesses where you can make hundreds of thousands of dollars a year as an immigrant without an expensive university education? Perhaps one could do so in the entertainment industry or with gambling or on Wall Street (another form of gambling), and none of these was promising to me.

Here is another tip

When I started out in real estate, I wrote a check to myself at the beginning of each year in the amount I wanted to make that year and put it in my wallet to follow my plan. And each year I met my goal. It was imprinted on my brain, and I worked to make it a reality. I always succeeded. It is a subconscious trick that worked for me. Perhaps you can try it, too. I increased the amount every year to a larger sum. I had started at $65,000 and leveled out at several hundred thousand dollars for years. I also made money from my investment remodeling jobs. When I finally let go of my license in Florida, I owned five investment properties in that state.

A suggestion: working as an assistant

To make the start in real estate easier at first, you could work as an assistant for a successful agent to learn the ropes and make an hourly wage. It is a good way to start in this business. Top agents are always looking for a helpful agent. You can call real estate offices and ask around about who is looking for an assistant. That will get your foot in the door, and you will get lots of experience. Top agents have dozens of listings and make over $300,000 a year in commissions; they need assistants to keep the ball rolling. Every office has top agents, so call and ask to find the one who wants to work with you. It is an easy way to start, and you get paid while learning.

When agents begin, they usually start with a fifty-fifty commission split with the company they work with. When they have achieved a certain level of sales, that commission is adjusted to a higher amount for the agent, a lesser one for the company. As I said before, the best agents make 85 percent, and the company makes 15 percent of their commissions. I was at the 85 percent level when I finally left California for Florida, thinking I could retire there. But I had to think again, because 2008 happened. I will get back to that later on in the hope that someone may learn and benefit from my experiences.

And now down to the facts of conducting real estate transactions; let us start with the obvious basics for agents, investors, and home owners alike.

CHAPTER 2

Sales, or purchase, contracts

T he purchase, or sales, contract for a property spells out in detail the offer a buyer is making to a seller. Items covered include price, terms of the contract, who represents whom, buyer or seller, amounts of money involved, the agency relationship with the agent/brokers, compensation to brokers, inspection clauses, date of proposed closing, contingencies, and so on.

Contracts can be signed in person or electronically today via programs like DocuSign. I recommend signing and explaining purchase contracts in person with your clients, unless you are dealing with a seasoned buyer or seller.

"The broker disclosure" spells out the agency relationship with the client, whether it is a "limited agency," "designated or single agency," "buyer's limited agency," "disclosed dual agency," or "transaction broker." The law allows licensees to enter into a variety of agency relationships with a client in a transaction. You need to understand the relationships of the parties with each other in a transaction. This needs to be spelled out in a written agreement, the "agency relationship disclosure."

All contracts need to spell out names of the parties involved in full, the purchase price offer, down payment and increase of deposit if any, balance of payment due at closing, contingencies (see below), and specific performance timelines—that is, expiration date and time of the offer. Contracts without names or signatures by all parties, or specific acceptance terms and dates, are noncontracts and cannot hold up in a court of law. They are a waste of time for everyone. So be very careful with your contracts!

Contingencies in a contract

There are several contingencies, which allow a buyer or seller to end a contract if they are not fulfilled. These are easy to understand and always the same.

1. *Financing contingency.* If the buyer fails to receive a loan commitment within the usually allowed thirty-day slot, the contract is voided and the buyer will receive a refund of his or her deposit.
2. *Appraisal contingency.* If the property does not appraise at the agreed-upon price, the buyer can void the contract or ask the seller to lower the price to the appraised value. If the seller refuses, the buyer can cancel the purchase offer.
3. *Home sale contingency.* If the buyer needs to sell a home in order to purchase the one he or she has made an offer on, this is spelled out clearly in the contract. A sale contingency is rarely accepted by a seller these days. If the buyer cannot sell the other property within the given time period, the contract ends.
4. *Title contingency.* If the seller cannot deliver a free and clear title of ownership for the desired property to the buyer, the contract ends. The buyer will not purchase the property. Should there be a "cloud" or "lien" on the

owner's title, such as a "mechanic's lien" for unpaid bills to a contractor or someone else's claim of ownership, the owner can and should remove those claims in order to close the sale. The title company researches the property to give a new owner right of ownerships that is free of any "encumbrances."

5. *Inspection contingencies*. The property should be inspected by the buyer's professional home inspector at the buyer's expense. If problems in the report arise, such as undisclosed items—for example, water in the basement during rains, mold on walls, broken pipes, no insulation in the attic, or wood-destroying infestations (termites)— the buyer can ask the seller to make the necessary repairs. The buyer can back out of the contract if the seller refuses. The buyer also has the option to ask for a reduction of price instead of repairs. Inspections are usually made within ten to fourteen days of the signing of the contract. If the home inspection turns up only minor defects, the buyer may decide to go ahead with the purchase anyway.

Home seller's disclosures

Every seller needs to complete a several-page-long disclosure form. In it all known facts about the property in question must be disclosed to the buyer, such as the age of the roof or whether any remodeling has been done with or without permits. All remodeling that involves plumbing, electrical wiring, load-bearing walls, etc., needs to be made with a permit. The city or county inspector (depending on the location of the property) will come and inspect the work after completion for correctness; otherwise, remodeling may cause future damage to a property, even including fires. A seller needs to disclose if there are any leakages, plumbing or electrical known defects, what kind of heating system is present, what type of plumbing the property has, whether the property has public water or a private well, whether the property is on a public sewer system or on its own septic tank, etc. A seller usually knows the property quite well and should be aware of any defects, such as structural problems or cracks in the foundations or walls, and has to disclose them.

No buyer should purchase a property without having examined the seller's disclosures in detail. Should the seller have omitted known facts and they become a problem during the buyer's professional inspections, the buyer now has recourse for remedy or a reduction of the price. This disclosure is very detailed and also contains neighborhood information. There are special pages that outline in detail which appliances will stay with the sale, what else will stay or go with the seller, and so on. As a buyer, examine the disclosures with a magnifying glass, so to speak!

Lead-based paint disclosures

The seller also has to sign and provide a "lead-based paint disclosure," including what he or she knows about lead-based paints in the building. Before 1978 paints contained lead, which is harmful when ingested or inhaled. Today no paints contain lead anymore; these disclosures are no longer required for homes built after 1978.

Condominium association disclosures

If the property is a condominium, the seller has to provide by law all disclosures a condo association keeps on file at all times; including monthly condo charges and what exactly these charges cover. The items covered usually include roof replacement/repair, building maintenance, possible swimming pool service, building insurance, hurricane or windstorm insurance, maintenance of grounds, electrical systems in common grounds, management fees and more. The association also has to provide financial statements, their yearly budget, disclosures about cash reserves, and a resale certificate.

If you purchase a condominium, you certainly want to know where all that money you pay goes every month. Some people like to live in condos, as they provide pool maintenance, snow removal, roof replacement, exterior painting maintenance, garbage removal, maintaining parking lots and driveways, and other benefits. They don't have to worry about any of it. It is all covered with one monthly fee.

However, buying a condominium as an investment requires special attention from you. The condo bylaws and rules and regulations may not allow rentals at all, or they may require a one-year owner occupancy before the condo can be rented out to tenants. Some will allow pets; others don't ever allow them, or they may allow pets up to a certain weight limit. It is also important to see if the association has plenty of cash reserves for repairs and maintenance. If there are no reserves or litigation is in process, you should stay away from such a condo development, as you would be buying into trouble. It is very important, therefore, that you ask for and receive all home owner association documents and review them thoroughly before you make an offer for a condo. Or if you have an offer written up, look at the documents immediately before you spend any money on inspections.

Good faith or earnest money deposits

An earnest money deposit in the form of a personal check or cashier's check is usually made with an offer and made out to the real estate brokerage or a title company. You should never hand cash to any agent. There is a timeline for additional deposits and final payment at closing. Contracts are getting longer and longer now. Years ago they were a few pages long; today they are at least six to ten pages. Well-paid attorneys have been working hard to think of everything that could possible go wrong with a deal and have added more paragraphs over time to avoid costly mistakes. That is a good thing; it will protect you and the client!

All you need to do is to read the contract carefully and explain it all to your client, and you don't need to worry about omitting important facts or making mistakes. It is all there and easy to follow. All real estate companies have these contracts on their computers for you to fill in, print out, and get signed—it's easy!

Lease/option purchase contracts

Plus two lease/option stories ...

Entering into a lease with an option to purchase a property can be two-edged sword. They are used from time to time when a buyer wishes to purchase a home but needs more time to accumulate enough funds to do so. The prospective buyer will rent the house he or she desires for an agreed-upon time, usually a year, and make a substantial, nonrefundable deposit at the beginning of the lease term to be then applied to the purchase price later on at closing. This deposit is usually 10 percent of the purchase price but is negotiable; a seller could ask for more than 10 percent. The seller can keep the deposit in full if the tenant/buyer cannot fulfill the contract, as the seller will now have lost a year of marketing time and possibly another buyer. This time delay could have serious consequences for the seller, as the market might have changed and the property might be worth more than the previously agreed-upon price.

The tenant/buyer has full possession of the property during the one-year period. There is the chance that he or she may damage the property or walk away after a year, with considerable repair costs awaiting the owner. I know of a case in which the tenant/option buyers had an expensive swimming pool built on the property and never paid a dime for it, claiming that they did not own the house. An inexperienced pool company fell for their story and actually built a huge pool, unbeknownst to the seller/owner. Perhaps the tenant had forged the owner's signatures with the pool contractors, but who knows? After not paying rent for a year, they then destroyed the pool and broke all tiles in it, stole all appliances from the house and everything else they could pack up, and disappeared with everything in the middle of the night. A bad story, but it happened.

Here is another cautionary story about a lease/option in Florida. Not knowing the real estate laws in this state, an owner had signed a lease/option contract with a couple and their unscrupulous agent for a nice home in a gated subdivision. The owner had received some minor option funds and the rent for two months; the price was set at $325,000 for a purchase a year later. All seemed fine.

One day, the owner drove by the property to check on it and saw a new For Sale sign on the front lawn. The owner was stunned, as he had not signed another listing contract with the same agent/broker. When he called her about the meaning of the sign, he was told that Florida law permits selling a property again under an option contract. The dual agent/broker now advertised the same house, still owned by the same original seller, for another $100,000, a price of $425,000. She stood to make a commission on the rental, the original option contract of a 5 percent commission for the sale price of $325,000, and another 5 or 6 percent commission on a possible new sale for $425,000, all at the same proposed closing!

The owner of the property contacted his attorney and reported the agent/broker to the ethics committee of the applicable Board of Realtors for unethical conduct. This broker would have lost her license had the tenants of the property not moved out and canceled all contracts with their unscrupulous agent. She did have the fiduciary duty to inform her client, the seller of the property, of all dealings and intended activity with his property as a dual agent, something she did not do, obviously. The owner of the home now had to find another tenant.

I know of one option to purchase contract that ended well. The payments were made to the seller by the prospective buyer in installments over a year, and the escrow closed when the buyer/tenant obtained a satisfactory purchase loan for the balance owed to the seller. The buyer was trustworthy, and the seller was experienced in real estate dealings. However, if you are a novice or have little experience in real estate, I would not recommend that you agree to any lease/option sales or purchases. There could be too many costly pitfalls.

CHAPTER 3

Property purchase loans and types of lenders

There are several type of lenders:

1. Visible lenders, including banks with a storefront such as Wells Fargo, Bank of America, and others you know. They have their own mortgage consultants who will sit in the bank and can get you a loan if you qualify.

2. Invisible ones such as wholesale lenders, which usually sit in an office in a high-rise building in New York, Los Angeles, or other big city. The average person will never set foot in a wholesale lender's office. However, they do lend money for real estate purchases, and mortgage brokers work mostly with these lenders. They used to offer better rates, as they don't have the overhead or expenses a bank has with a storefront and the expenses of a large bank building. These lenders are also underwritten (guaranteed or insured) by the government institutions Fannie Mae and Freddie Mac. Since 2008, many wholesale lenders have fallen by the wayside and no longer operate, but some are back in business again. As I said, mortgage brokers work mostly with these wholesale lenders, and

they may approve a loan for you that a conventional bank wouldn't.

3. For more information about Fannie Mae and Freddie Mac, go to www.google.com and research these government agencies under the Federal Housing Finance Agency (FHFA) for maximum loan amounts allowed in various states of the country. Fannie Mae will guarantee "conforming" loan amounts up to a certain level (in some states at $417,000 now), and Freddie Mac loans above the conforming amounts, or "jumbo" loans. Jumbo loans usually have higher interest rates.

4. "Hard money lenders" are companies that will lend you money for a real estate purchase or business venture at very high (usury) rates, because you cannot get money from anyone else. They will secure their money with a lien on your property or other assets you may have. Mortgage brokers have access to these lenders.

5. Private lenders are single, private persons who will lend you money at very high rates and who will also place a lien on your property.

"Creative" financing before 2008

Before the crash of 2008/2009 there were many "creative financing" possibilities. Some lenders would give a first and a second loan on the same property at exorbitant interest rates to help people into home ownership. Some gave 100 percent financing, "no-money-down" loans, again with punishing interest rates around 10 percent or more. Most people could not afford these loans. Lenders were creating an artificial financial and real estate landscape that was destined to failure from the start. Banks raked in a huge amount of money in interest payments and penalties. Some lenders gave loans to people who had no source of income; in other words, you could buy a house without a job to make the payments, based on some funds in the bank and a promise in writing.

There were 3 percent down payments with large mortgage insurance payments, 5 percent down payments, 10 and 15 percent down payments, and even placing a lien on another property the buyer might own to secure the present purchase. Anything was possible. The banks knew they would always get the properties back should the buyers fail. And fail they did, as we all know now. But the dream of home ownership was alluring and very much promoted by the banks.

To make matter worse, many loans were given with "negative amortization," which meant, in a nutshell, that after you made payments faithfully for ten years, you would still owe practically the same amount or more to the bank and had not paid down your principal loan amount at all. It was outrageous and yet very popular because the interest rates were lower than others. These loans were taken out by people who did not intend to keep a property for long, perhaps two or three years, and then sell it for a profit. They certainly did not intend to keep these houses for thirty years. In the meantime, until they would sell, their mortgage payments were very low. That made sense then, but when the market crashed, they were stuck with these terrible loans and properties they could no longer sell. When they stopped the payments and walked away from these properties, the underwriting government insurance entities such as Fannie Mae and Freddie Mac were now also stuck with millions of these properties, which they are now slowly selling off as REOs (bank-owned) and foreclosures.

Had the lenders not offered these terrible loans, people would not have bought and the crash may not have occurred? I do fault the lenders for their greed, as most people do. And yet the government bailed them out with taxpayers' money to avoid another worldwide depression!

Thankfully, today these shady lending practices are a thing of the past. To purchase any property today, and in order for a lender or mortgage broker to give you a purchase money mortgage, you should have a sizable non-borrowed down payment of 20 percent or more and proof of where that money came from with a paper trail. Lenders now offer 3 percent down and 5 percent down payment loans again, but you need to have excellent credit with a super high FICO score (see chapter 6 for credit reports) or more to be approved for such a loan. Interest rates are more reasonable now, around 4.5 percent for a purchase or even less.

You also have to show the lender that you have enough income each month to make the payments without stress; the payments should be about 30 percent of your income. Thankfully, the mortgage lending practices are back to a normal level.

Home equity loans

Should you have plenty of equity in your home—let us say 50 percent of the appraised value or more (it depends on the lender how much equity they will look for)—a home equity loan can help you in different ways. With such a loan at today's more reasonable rates, you can cash out a certain amount of money to use for various purposes. And the interest you pay on the equity loan is always tax deductible! Here are some examples for the use of a cash or equity line of credit:

1. Home improvements that will raise the value of the property and make a future sale more promising with a higher sales price.

2. You can consolidate your credit card debts into one home equity loan payment, which is tax deductible as mentioned above, whereas your credit card payments are not deductible. It would be a good idea to close your credit card accounts after paying them off to avoid more debts in the future.

3. You can pay off your own or your children's college education loan and give them a debt-free start in life.

Reverse mortgages

If you are over sixty-two and your home is all paid off, and you may have a budget squeeze or want to go on that around-the-world cruise, you may want to consider a reverse mortgage. It is legitimate and a great help to older people who may be running out of money and are outliving their savings. The lender will appraise your home and pay you a monthly amount without your having to pay interest. The value of the home declines according to the payments you receive, and ... well, you will leave less to your relatives or kids, but you can greatly improve your lifestyle without worrying where the next dollar for food is coming from. You should get a reverse mortgage only from a reputable lender, of course; that is, a bank you can walk into, as they will place a lien on your house to secure the reverse mortgage.

A friend of mine had her house appraised at $425,000 during the height of the market before 2008, when in fact it was a row house in an over-fifty-five community in a subdivision in Florida. It was really worth $175,000 at my best guess. She was approved for a reverse mortgage with rather large up-front fees and soon was receiving monthly payments of over $2000. That came in handy, as she had just been diagnosed with a debilitating illness at age seventy-two and needed the funds for her treatments. However, when values sharply declined after 2008, her home might have been reappraised by the same lender. I hope for her sake that she is still continuing to receive her payments and did not lose her home, too.

çLynette Yencho

VA loans

The government provides 100 percent financing for veterans who wish to purchase a home, which is a great advantage for returning soldiers and their families. The Veterans Administration work with lenders to give veterans loans at very reasonable rates without a down payment. Every month the buyers will pay the property taxes and insurance together with their interest payment and the payment toward the principle. People can obtain only one VA loan at a time, and they have to live on the property. These loans are not available for investments.

CHAPTER 4

Escrows and settlement statements

An escrow is opened when an agent accepts a deposit check from a buyer who wants to purchase a certain property. The check is made out to the real estate company the agent works with or to a title company.

This deposit is held "in escrow" until a sales contract has been signed and all conditions in the contract have been accepted by both parties, seller and buyer, and all contingencies have been removed. You now have an active escrow.

Price, timing, and conditions of the sale/purchase are laid out in the contract with specific time limitations. The deposit is a part of the purchase or sales price. Usually another deposit is made after contingencies have been removed by both parties in writing. Contingencies are inspections of the property and/or obtaining a mortgage by the buyer. Once those conditions have been fulfilled within a given time limit, buyer and seller go to a "closing," which takes place at a title company.

Usually the seller chooses the title or escrow company. Here the final documents are signed. There are many title companies in the country; some are owned by large real estate corporations.

A few names that come to mind are First American Title Co., Continental Title Co., and Chicago Title Co.

If the buyer cannot obtain a loan or is dissatisfied with the inspections, the deposit check is returned to the buyer and there is no sale. The escrow is canceled in writing by all parties.

If sailing is smooth, the transaction will close on the designated day. The seller will have sold his or her property, and the buyer will have purchased a home. The title company will issue a check to the seller for his or her proceeds and sales commission checks for the agents. The commission checks will go to the agent's brokerage, and then the agents will be paid their percentages of the commissions by the brokers according to the contracts the brokers have with them.

The title company prepares the settlement statements, which clearly spell out who pays what and how much in a transaction. The final settlement statement is called the **HUD-1;** by federal law of the Department of Housing and Urban Development, both the seller and the buyer should receive a copy of the HUD-1 well before the day of settlement. They need to know what they can expect to pay and/or receive at closing.

If you don't receive such a preliminary closing statement, ask for it; *never* go to a closing without having examined your statement first. It is the law, as I said!

Changes occur in the industry all the time, and in California the buyer and the seller now receive separate statements—so the buyer cannot see the seller's proceeds at closing, for example. Today's privacy laws forbid that the buyer should know how large a mortgage the seller is paying off at closing or what other debts he or she may be paying off and/or how much of a gain they realize with a sale. And it is really none of the buyer's business.

Just a few years ago, in the settlement statements for a buyer and a seller in the same transaction, all amounts were shown on one large document even in California. That is still the case in many other states.

If a purchase does not work out, an escrow has to be canceled in writing and signed by all parties to refund the buyer's deposit by the title company that is holding it in escrow.

Seller's closing costs

The seller's closing costs will be the mortgage payoff and bank fee, if there is loan; possible prepayment penalties (check your loan; you can do so online); recording fees; commissions to all agents involved in the transaction; notary fees; and escrow and title fees. Sometimes a seller will buy a home warranty for a buyer. The amounts of a seller's costs can vary depending on the value of the home he or she is selling; however, they are usually less than a buyer's fees.

Buyer's closing costs

The buyer's closing costs include the additional agreed-upon down payment; funds from a lender giving a loan if there is one; title insurance fee; escrow fee; possible points to the lender; possible first three months' mortgage payment if the down payment is less than 20 percent; possible mortgage insurance; possible reserve bank payments; prepaid HOA fees if it is condo; possible home warranty cost if the buyer wants one; and always recording fees at the county courthouse for future property tax assessments. A buyer's closing costs are usually between 2 and 3 percent of the purchase price.

The title company will figure all these costs out on the HUD-1, and all parties need to scrutinize the statement carefully. But they rarely make mistakes. Only once a title company overcharged me by $350; they added the escrow fee twice. That is not much in twenty years of closings.

Escrow or transaction calendars for agents

A transaction calendar is an enormous help to an agent. I made one for each contract I was working on in order to keep on top of the various dates in it. If you have several transactions going on at the same time, it is otherwise impossible to keep the various dates straight in your mind. I attached the calendar for additional deposits, contingency removals, etc., to the inside of each file for easy access and checked them off as we progressed.

Many agents, even those who have been in business for years, allow transactions to fall apart if they are not careful and don't have the skills to close the deal. That happens all the time. Even a seasoned agent, not paying attention to the timeline of a trans-action, might allow a sale to slip away. Often buyers, as well as sellers, experience remorse ("buyer's remorse" or "seller's re-morse"), a temporary emotional setback that usually passes. A good agent will keep his or her thumbs on the deal, check the written timeline every day to make sure all dates and contingen-cies of the contract are adhered to by both parties, and ensure that the necessary documents are signed. One slip on the contract by the agent would allow a seller to get out of the sales contract, and the buyer could walk away without legal ramifications. This is a bad idea, as the buyer or seller usually regret the decision later and then have to start all over again, which is a time-consuming process, to say the least.

And you, the agent, will find yourself without a closing and many wasted hours of work—not a situation any agent would want. So keep those transaction calendars going with diligence!

I also kept records of all writings, e-mails, and phone calls with my clients for future reference. Keeping track is easy; just don't delete them on your iPhone or computer and/or iPad until after the deal has closed and allow a few extra weeks in case some problems should appear later.

CHAPTER 5

Becoming a real estate investor

R eal estate investing is where you can make the big bucks!

I believe that if you don't want to be an agent and never work under a broker, and you just want to work as a real estate investor, it is best to gain experience by working as an agent before you become an investor and buy, fix up, and sell (or "flip") properties. Again, make a plan to follow and learn the ground rules. Decide where in the country you want to work, if you have a choice. Obviously it is better to work in an affluent neighborhood or a wealthy part of the country than in a poor one. Pricing is higher and therefore profits are better, as well. If you work in a part of the country where the minimum price of a house is $500,000, your gain will be higher than if you work in an area where the average house price is $50,000. It is just common sense. For example, if you buy a property at foreclosure for $125,000 and the neighborhood values are around $600,000, and you put another $150,000 into improvements and the house looks great, you stand to make a nice profit of $325,000 when you sell it again. That's not bad for a few months' work! If you buy such a great opportunity at an auction, you will need some cash for the purchase at the auction (usually 10 percent of the sales price), and you have to be able to get a loan for the difference within thirty days or pay the balance in cash.

People in wealthier neighborhoods can afford to buy more expensive homes and also can pay higher rent, if you want to rent out investment properties. I happened to live and work in a very affluent part of California and later in Palm Beach County, Florida, where real estate values are high and therefore income possibilities are higher, as well.

Here are the rules for success:

Rule # 1: Location, location, location

It is the one everyone has heard of … it's still true today and always will be. Whether you buy a property for yourself to live in or one to invest in, location is the most important factor in real estate.

The smallest house in the best neighborhood is always a better choice over the largest house in the lesser neighborhood. Often people get tempted to buy the white elephant in a less desirable or poor neighborhood, because it is cheaper than other large homes elsewhere. Don't succumb to the temptation—never! You will have trouble selling it again for sure, and it will lose value over time. The smaller home in the better neighborhood is a much better bet. It will keep its value. Perhaps you can add on to the existing structure for more space, and at least you will always be able to rent it out.

A story about locations

Here is the story about locations that happened to me personally. I was new to Florida and wanted to buy a home to live in. One day I saw a wonderful Spanish-style courtyard home advertised in a real estate magazine. It was located in a development that was a golfing community. I drove to the sales office and was shown the lovely home in this gated community. It was just what I wanted, with the inner pool courtyard for privacy, and it had a guest cottage for my visiting family and friends. I was so excited about the house that I told a neighbor about it. He exclaimed: "Did you drive around the back of the development?!" When I said, "No, I did not," he continued to tell me that there was a garbage dump behind the development. The day I visited, the wind had not been blowing the toxic fumes in my direction, and the dump had gone unnoticed. I returned to the sales office and voiced my opinion. Then I drove back around the development and saw the huge county dump right there! Had I purchased, I would have sat on my beautiful patio and breathed in the smell and toxic gas of the dump every day! My neighbor had clued me in, and I thanked him! He had nearly purchased there himself.

The message to you is to investigate all areas around a property you wish to purchase in any neighborhood. Do not rely on the advertising or brochures about any property. Be your own investigator, always!

Rule #2: Research the property

Get all the information you need about any property you are interested in before making an offer. Besides what is available already about the property from the website, agent, or listing information, research it at the county courthouse. Records are available there on *any* property in any county, such as size of lot, zoning for residential use or commercial use or multiple uses, tax assessments, and property value according to the tax assessor's evaluation. The tax assessor's value shown is, thankfully, always lower than the market value. You will also find out if the present owner is behind in property tax payments or not, the value of neighboring properties, and other facts about the property. This is a source of very important information. You can obtain this by either going to the courthouse in person or obtaining it through the Internet by going to, for example, www.johnsoncounty.org or www.jacksoncounty. org. It is all public information.

Rule #3: Get an inspection

Do not let a real estate salesperson talk you into a purchase. Some agents can be very persuasive and flattering, particularly if they need to make a commission to pay their upcoming bills. Do your research, examine the house you are interested in very carefully, and *always* get a professional inspection of the property, plus a termite inspection if it is a wooden construction or has wooden trusses, and also a roof inspection if part of the roof is not visible. This will be money well spent to avoid costly mistakes and/or repairs. This is true for your own home purchase to live in, as well as for investment properties, and the inspection(s) will help you figure out your total costs for the intended purchase.

Here is something to learn from:

Despite all my twenty years of experience, I purchased a house once without a home inspection, because I really wanted to buy it and wanted it fast! And guess what happened after the move-in— the seller had not disclosed all the negative facts about the house in the seller's disclosures. I was standing in the garage one day, and the plumbing overhead gave way (it was rotted out on top where it was not visible), and the whole mess poured down onto me and my car. An inspector would have found the problem, and it was an expensive mistake to have made.

All agents have names of inspectors they can recommend to you, and the Board of Realtors in your town also has a list of names, or you can Google them. Paying for a home inspection is money well spent and helps one avoid regrets.

You can find business cards from inspectors and other real estate–related businesses in every Board of Realtors office in every part of the country and in every town. Every town has its own Board of Realtors where Realtors meet. They usually display many of these business cards, including those of mortgage brokers and insurance brokers. Or you can just go to the Internet.

A big *no-no*: agents don't do inspections!

Some agents I came across took it upon themselves to inspect a property for their clients. They would inspect the interior and the exterior of a house, though no one expected it. I have seen one agent even climb on a roof, endangering his life, and crawl into an attic. That was quite stupid and, furthermore, completely uncalled for. I guess he wanted to impress his clients. Only licensed inspectors should inspect homes. An agent should be there and perhaps take notes, and the agent is allowed to verbally point out easily visible defects to his or her client. Today inspectors will give you a computer-generated and typed written report on the property after they finish their work, right on the spot. If an agent becomes involved in the process and makes statements about the condition of the property, he or she could be subject to a lawsuit. It is much easier and safer to stay out of the inspection process. The agent simply reads the report and hands it to the buyer and seller and perhaps helps with a price negotiation should the report show that work is required on the house.

An annoying inspection story

In California I once sold a house to a couple of women, and they waived the right to inspections. I was the listing and the selling agent in a dual, disclosed agency. Everything went well, and the sale closed. A week or so later I received a call from one of the women. Apparently some bathroom pipes that went under the house into the crawl space (California has no basements, just crawl spaces under houses) were lying on the ground and were not connected to the sewage system in the road. These women had waived the right to inspections, but they now accused me of not disclosing the condition of the plumbing. I had no obligation to crawl under the house to look at pipes and sewer connections. No agent will ever do that! But my broker at the time took $4,000 out of my commission to pay the women. My guess is that they looked at how much I had made on the sale and decided to get some of that money for themselves, though the seller had paid the commission.

You win some and you lose some, but this was a raw deal and I was more than annoyed! The company could have afforded to pay for the damage rather than take it from me. I did not stay much longer with that company!

Rule #4: Get an appraisal

"A house is worth what a buyer is willing to pay."

Yes and no! Before 2008, when real estate took a huge tumble and values fell by 50 percent in some areas—like Las Vegas in Nevada, and Florida—mortgage brokers could get you a loan on borrowed down payments and false income statements. Banks were very lenient and overlooked many statements on loan applications that should have been red flags to them. People made income statements that were not factual. Loans were made on "stated income" and three months of bank statements. Heavy fees and points (a point is 1 percent of the loan amount) were charged, often as much as 3 percent or more up front, when the actual income of the person did not support the mortgage payment and other expenses for the property. The lenders were interested in reaping the income and up-front buyer's costs they could get from these loans, and then they sold them off to the secondary market at a discount.

These practices, of course, helped lead to the collapse of the housing market and the downfall of some Wall Street banks and investments companies, as was mentioned before. To make matters worse, appraisers that worked for the lenders appraised the properties at inflated prices; they usually arrived miraculously at the contract price by manipulating the values, picking properties for comparisons that were not in the same area or that had been sold much longer ago than the six months' time period usually required for comparisons by a lender. I have seen comparisons (or "comps," for short) vary by tens of thousands of dollars or more for the same property. It was amazing. One property I sold had appraisals ranging from $550,000 to $800,000! Figure it out! I couldn't!

It is therefore very important to get an honest appraisal from an independent appraiser, or even several appraisers, before you purchase a high-priced property, as the risk is higher for overpaying. Again, good sources to search for an appraiser would be the Internet or your local Board of Realtors. The lender will send their own appraiser while the loan is in underwriting, to arrive at an appraised value to substantiate the loan. These appraisers usually only do a "drive-by" and never see the inside of the property. It is therefore always prudent to get your own independent appraisal for comparison, as well.

Real estate agents often supply you with comparison charts of houses sold in your chosen area and neighborhood for the last six months. This called a comparative market analysis, or CMA. Lenders also use a CMA to arrive at a loan amount they are willing to give you, of course. If you work with an agent, you should ask that agent for such an analysis before you make any decision at all. Agents have this information readily available on their computers. It takes only a few moments to download a CMA and hand it to you. Every buyer and seller should always have a CMA to study in detail.

Today, lenders are much stricter, with tighter underwriting rules, and relying on stated incomes on mortgage applications is a thing of the past, thankfully. I do believe that, had the banks appraised properties not at the inflated prices as they did before 2008, but at their real value, many people would have kept their homes. They would not have been tempted to "upgrade" to a larger home they could not afford. But they were misled by lenders and mortgage brokers with the "stated income" loan applications. These were treacherous, and people purchased properties they could not afford at all. On top of that, the banks told them the properties were worth the price they were willing to pay, when the houses were totally overpriced. If the banks' appraisers had not supported the false house pricing and banks had not ap-proved loans to people without sufficient income to make the required payments, many buyers would not have bought and the collapse might not have occurred. As it was, millions of homes went into foreclosure because of the banks' terrible and greedy lending procedures.

Rule #5: No borrowed down payment

Never purchase a property with a borrowed down payment. It may be too difficult to pay both the mortgage and the loan for the down payment, plus other ordinary living expenses. Lenders usually did not allow borrowed down payments even before 2008 and certainly don't allow them today. The funds in your account had to be "seasoned" only for at least three months before 2008, but now you have to prove where the funds are coming from with a long paper trail.

Therefore, have your funds in your account for at least six months, plus documentation of where the funds came from, before you make a purchase. Real estate is not a getting-rich-over-night game; you have to know the rules and apply them, but if you do, you will get there for sure. Of course, if you pay cash, you don't have to worry about any of this.

Rule # 6: Don't rely on the seller

This is a very basic rule: never buy a property from a seller based on the seller's "good word"; always get a title company to do the closing for you and get the proper title search done, and get title insurance, your inspections, and an appraisal. This process is worth every penny you spend on it. Of course a real estate attorney can handle a purchase or sale for you as well.

CHAPTER 6

The importance of credit reports

If you need financing, the most important factor in purchasing real estate besides your purchase funds is your FICO score and/or credit report. The FICO score is arrived at from pooling all three reports from the existing three credit companies. These companies are as follows:

TransUnion, Experian, and Equifax

Every one of your financial actions—such as applying for a card, a loan you take out, and you miss—is reflected on your credit report. Some companies report to only one of the three; some report to all three. Your FICO score is based on your outstanding debt versus payments you made. All your debts are listed here except for private loans you may have. If you are more than sixty days late on one of your payments, it will show up as a sixty days late on your report. The number of "lates" and all on-time payments are computed, and the result is your creditworthiness as a FICO score. A score under 600 is considered quite bad, a score around 500 is not at all creditworthy, and a score over 700 is good. Lenders look for scores over 700 to over 800.

If you have a great credit score, you will be given a loan if you can support the payments with your income. Strangely enough, it does not matter how much money you have in the bank at the time of the application. The banks figure you could lose it all in Las Vegas!

You have one free credit check per year with any of the three companies. You need to sign up for a year, though, to get it. I just cancel the subscription after I have my information and get my free report. There are other companies offering free credit reports such as www.freecreditreport.com. Discover card will give you your free FICO score as a service to their credit card holders.

If you find your credit is bad, there are companies that can help you fix it up. Again, you need to search on Google for credit repair companies. Often negative reports were not lifted after a debt was actually paid, or an erroneous report showed up somehow. These companies specialize in fixing such errors. Also, some negative information needs to be removed by law after so many years, such as court judgments or liens. You need a specialist to help you with these issues.

If you have no credit at all, apply for a credit card, purchase a few items, and pay the bills immediately to establish credit. Everyone living in these times needs to have credit. Without it you cannot purchase real estate ... except for cash, of course.

CHAPTER 7

Fixing up houses and capital gains tax-free earnings

On top of commissions I earned, I made money fixing up houses in California, usually the ones I lived in, plus some investment properties in Florida later on. My last sale in Florida was for $799,000, and I had paid $575,000 for it. The events of 2008 and the drop in real estate values made it necessary for me to live in that property and wait for a better price much longer than I had planned to. But I finally sold it and realized a $224,000 gain. The present federal tax laws allow you to remodel and fix up a house and then sell it with a profit capital gains tax break, if you live in the house for two years out of five. You don't have to live there for five years, just two full years. You can rent out the house for the other three years if you wish, although you will have to pay tax at the rate of 25 percent on any depreciation that you claimed during the rental period of time. These are the present tax laws; however consult with your accountant as these laws may change.

This requirement, of course, means that you have to move every few years, but if the gain is large enough it might be worthwhile. As a married person you have a $500,000 tax-free gain, and as a single person you have a $250,000 tax-free gain with today's tax laws. I believe that such a tax-free gain makes it worthwhile to move, even if you have other substantial income. You can keep your furnishings and belongings to a minimum and make the moving process easier.

For example, I purchased a house for $450,000 with a 20 percent down payment, fixed it up, decorated it, and sold it later for $1 million and paid no capital gains tax on the sale. I was married and had a $500,000 tax-free gain deduction. I also deducted the improvement costs. However, you do not have to spend much to make money in real estate, nor do you need a license as a real estate professional to flip houses. You can buy cheaper, fore-closed properties right now, fix them up, and sell them again for a gain anywhere in the country. But it takes some research from you and knowledge about the real estate market. If you buy and "flip" houses within a few months without occupying them for at least two years, you will have to pay the current capital gains tax which is 15 percent or 20 percent, depending on your overall tax bracket. There may also be a 3.8 percent investment tax for payers with a high adjusted gross income. Please consult with your tax advisor and /or accountant. In addition I advise you to get your real estate license first before you invest in real estate.

The best time to buy investment properties is right now

There has never been a better time to buy properties. Money is virtually lying in the streets to be picked up. Why? Well, the banks have foreclosed on thousands and thousands of homes all over the country since 2008. That process is still going on. It has not stopped by any means; people are still struggling to keep their homes, are losing their jobs, and are unable to afford the payments they signed up for. The banks are sitting on millions of foreclosed properties all over the country at this time. They are releasing them slowly, one by one, as REO (bank-owned) fore-closed properties or by auction right now and will be doing so for a long time to come. There are that many homes available, and they eventually need to be sold by the lenders so that the banks can recoup some of their losses.

You can find these properties on many websites: www.Auction.com, www.Trulia.com, www.Zillow.com and sometimes www.realtor.com, www.HomePath.com (Fannie Mae properties), www.HomeSteps.com (Freddie Mac properties), www.RealtyBid.com, www.RealtyTrac.com, and more. Some of these sites are available as apps on most mobile devices so that you can do research anywhere you have Internet access. Zillow.com is now in the process of buying out Trulia.com.

Please note that all Homepath properties must be owner-occupied for at least a year or there is a large penalty you may have to pay. After occupying a Homepath property for the one year you can then rent it out or sell it. If you are the daring type you could remodel the property or fix it up for resale during that year as well.

You need to sift through the listings on the various websites one by one and find something in your cash payment price range and in your neighborhood or close to it to avoid long-distance commuting to the property.

Again, it is important to pay attention to the location. A house close to the freeway will be tougher to sell again, as will a house next to railroad tracks. I stay away from homes next to main traffic roads, as well. Most people don't like traffic noise, not to mention the pollution the passing cars will emit. These properties may also be subject to "eminent domain," which means the government authorities have the right to ask you to sell them the property for a nominal reimbursement to widen roads and highways or to build new freeways right over your property.

You can start your investment career with an inexpensive property, of course. It does not have to be an expensive house at first. Buy a smaller house with a smaller down payment, or pay cash if you can. If you want to live in it for two years or more, begin at what you can afford with a 20 percent down payment. If you make a smaller down payment of 3 percent or 5 percent you will incur very high closing costs; such as mort-   gage insurance; prepayments of your mortgage for   a few months; and property tax reserve payments; plus you will have a higher interest rate. In my opinion that is not the best way to start out with a first home purchase. You will be better off to save up a 20 percent down payment and not incur the penalties which the banks will greatly benefit from. Make your monthly mortgage payments, fix the house up nicely, and decorate it; then sell it after the two years for a nice profit. If you borrow the down payment from family or friends, make sure it shows up in your account long before you contact a bank for a purchase loan. As was mentioned before, the lenders will check where the money came from, and they will check your income

© Lynette Yencho

sources and ability to pay back the loan, plus check your credit reports.

Here is a word of advice about buying foreclosures online from www.auction.com. Sometimes these properties are *not* listed with an agent. You will not have access to the inside of a property in that case. Auction.com offers properties all over the United States. Chances are you'll find some in your neighborhood. If you are interested in one of those properties go to see it, look at the neighborhood, walk behind the house, peek through the windows, they are usually vacant. You will have a pretty good impression of the value of that property.

Never, absolutely never buy any property if you cannot view at least part of the interior. The reason for this warning is obvious: the remodeling can cost you much more than the property will ever be worth, and you can lose your shirt, no matter how low and interesting the price might seem. Here is an example: You buy a foreclosure for $100,000. It needs tons of work in the amount of another $100,000 by the time you finish, but the area values are only $150,000. You have just made a financial hole for yourself in the amount of $50,000. You may never be able to recoup that!

Cash owner-occupied purchases

If you can pay cash for a property, so much the better. There will be no need for bank applications for a loan, no one will check your credit, and you can close fast, usually within two weeks for a cash purchase.

Title companies will require that much time to search the title for the property to make sure it is clear and free of encumbrances or liens from other people or contractors who may have performed work on the property previously and placed a mechanic's lien on the property if they did not get paid. A lien on a property means that they will be able to collect and get paid at closing, when the property title transfers to a new person. Should someone purchase that property, the buyer may have to pay the mechanic's lien.

The title company will do the research at the county courthouse to make sure the property is free of any liens (that there is no "cloud on the title" or "encumbrances"), so that they can issue a title report and insure the title, giving you complete and free ownership. That will usually take two weeks.

Cash non-owner-occupied investments (fixers)

If you have the means, you can purchase a house with cash, fix it up, and sell it for a profit whenever you want to, but you will have to pay capital gains tax, presently at 15 or 20 percent, depending on your adjusted gross income. If you flip properties constantly and that is your business, you may have to pay an additional tax which could be another 15 percent. This is the new social security tax which became effective in 2014.

Please consult with your tax accountant or attorney regarding this new tax law. If you have a small spread between your purchase and sales price, such as $20,000, the flipping deal may not be worthwhile for all the work that is involved after paying commissions and expenses.

However, if you have a few hundred thousand dollars of gain, paying 15 or 20 percent tax to Uncle Sam on your gain may still be worth the work you did. In addition there may be a 3.8 percent investment tax.

Please consult with your accountant or tax attorney, as your taxation will vary according to your overall income and on how often you flip a property. But for many small investors, the IRS just closed the door to making some smaller profits in real estate within short periods of time. However, you can still purchase a foreclosure or short sale, rent it out for a couple of years, fix it up, and then sell it later on. But flipping an inexpensive property within a few months is no longer as attractive as it used to be.

Deferring capital gains or 1031 exchanges

Uncle Sam provides another opportunity for investors of real estate in the form of what is called a 1031 exchange, provided by Internal Revenue Code section 1031. This strategy allows you to delay the payment of the capital gains by deferring it and not paying at the time of the sale. This is a very useful tool for investors and probably not used often enough, as many people are not aware of it. It is only useful if you actually realize a gain from the sale of a property. You can roll this gain over to another property, but it must be a like-kind property and within the United States. You cannot sell something in the US and roll the gain over to a property in another country. The IRS would not allow it.

In other words, you can defer payment of the capital gains taxes by buying another like-kind property, i.e. a town home purchased for investment to another investment home or town home or even land. You cannot exchange gains from the sale of an apartment building to stocks or bonds, it must be real property. There are several other conditions for a deferred exchange to be allowed by the IRS.

1. A qualified exchange intermediary needs to be chosen before the closing of the first property that will hold the

funds from the sale. Any funds diverted from the proceeds will be taxed at regular capital gains taxation rates. (Consult with your accountant).

2. This chosen 1031 exchange specialist—such as OREXCO—will not only hold the funds, but also prepare all documents according to the requirements of the IRS and assist with the new closing through a title company or real estate attorney. Some title companies are also qualified as intermediaries, as are some real estate attorneys. They will prepare an exchange agreement, an assignment of the sales contract and will provide the escrow or closing agent with the required documentation.

3. You need to identify several other new replacement properties from the date of closing of the first property and do so within forty five days after closing and in writing to the intermediary.

4. You need to purchase one of the identified replacement properties and close within 180 days after the closing of the first property. You may not purchase a property that was not previously identified by you. The exchange would be voided.

The IRS 1031 exchanges can be complex, so please consult with your tax attorney or accountant about this matter before engaging in an exchange. The internet also provides further information if you research it. Google "Internal Revenue Code section 103".

These exchanges allow you to defer your gain - if you have one - and possibly for many years. There is some work involved in this process, but it is a very useful tool for investors and is allowed by Uncle Sam.

Obviously there is no need for a 1031 exchange if you incur a loss at the sale of an investment property.

Advice about tenants and renting a property out

However, purchasing an investment property to rent out will give you a much larger return of income on your money than you will get in interest from banks. Money market accounts had fallen by the wayside for years after 2008. Now you can get a money market account again, but the interest is only 0.05 percent at most banks or even less at this time. For example, if you buy a rental house for $70,000 and get $700 per month in rent your return will be 12 percent per year. An easy choice for most people even after deducting property tax expenses, insurance costs and a yearly 5 percent vacancy factor of the rent (at $700 rent it is $35), plus possible repairs. You will be better off than with leaving your money in a bank account and receiving next to nothing in interest. Furthermore, real estate is a tangible asset.

In addition to a better return on your funds, your tenant will help pay down your mortgage with his rent payments and over time properties usually increase in value if they are kept up well. Furthermore you can deduct rental property taxes, insurance and repairs from your regular income; a large bonus from Uncle Sam.

Of course, you have to screen your tenants very carefully. *Always* ask for a credit report, proof of employment and references you can contact (make sure it is not their mother). Without these three items you should not rent to anyone. You can purchase leases at OfficeMax or OfficeDepot or ask your real estate attorney to draw up a good residential lease to protect you. The latter would be the better choice as your attorney will protect your interests and know the local laws. In addition, *always* get a substantial security deposit. I ask for at least one month's rent security payment or preferably one and a half or two months, in addition to the usual first and last month's rent.

If the tenant damaged your property you can and should use their security deposit to make repairs or paint the walls, replace carpeting. You need to inform your tenant about your intention to retain their deposit or a part of it. Take photos of the damage for proof. Each state has specific tenant/landlord laws to follow. You can also lease out your property with the assistance of a real estate agent who will do the necessary paperwork for you.

Never rent out a property without a security deposit. If there is no damage, you have to refund the entire amount within a time frame specified by law, usually 30 days. This may differ from state to state. A security deposit needs to be kept in a separate account (an escrow account) and cannot be co-mingled with personal funds.

You don't need a real estate license to purchase and fix up, rent and sell, though I always recommend that you do get a license to gain a basic understanding and knowledge of the market, as I said before.

And you also need knowledge of neighborhood and location values, and the prices similar homes sold for in the prior six months. These are fundamental must-do items you should never buy and sell any property without. Get the needed information about the property at your county courthouse or from your Realtor.

To improve and fix up a property and to gain knowledge in the marketplace about decorating trends, go to open houses in the area and observe how they are decorated. Visit more upscale homes and look at their bathrooms, kitchens, and other parts of the house to get a feel for what is presently "in", as far as ambiance and presentation. Do not rely on your own personal tastes! You may think you have good taste, when in fact others may not agree.

I recently saw a house with silver-engraved metal backsplashes behind the black counters in the kitchen. Perhaps the owners thought it was "cool," but in fact it was not attractive to me personally. Other houses I saw had garish colors on the walls, which might clash with the furniture colors of new owners. Stay neutral and light in your decor. Dark brown wooden cabinets in kitchens or dark paneled walls in any room in a house are no longer in vogue at this time. Kitchens are light or even white again. Look at magazines that display home decor. Paint dark brown panels a light, neutral color, and the whole room will be brighter. It is best to use really good paint, like Sherwin-Williams paints. Cheap paints may chip and peel off very soon.

Staging a property for sale

Staging or decorating a property is extremely important if you want to make money in real estate. Without that you may fail, so please trust me on this issue. This holds true for your own investments, or for your sellers if you are an agent. You can and should advise your sellers about this important fact.

The eye of a buyer will decide in the first few minutes of entering a property if they like it or not. The first few minutes are crucial. I have looked at a property from the outside only and said no. Or I have gone inside a house and immediately said no or yes. First impressions count; they are *most* important!

The front of a house should be landscaped at least, and it should have an inviting front door. If the paint on the front door is peeling or the door has been bashed in, a potential buyer might keep driving and not be tempted to look at the inside of the house. Plants and flowers in the front of a property make it friendlier and nice look-ing. Inside, fresh paint and clean car-pets and windows make a huge dif-ference and don't cost a lot. Flowers in vases inside a home make it look friend-lier and add a touch of class.

If you are a smoker, very definitely get rid of the smoke smell and always, always use an air freshener to get rid of unpleasant odors.

©Lynette Yencho

Most of the time, if you choose your list-ings with care—do the research about price and loca-tion—any house will sell in a decent market, which we are slowly getting back to again. Sometimes it takes longer; sometimes you need to reduce the price. And always hold open houses. I've sold many houses on the first or second open house. They are also a very good way to meet neighbors and get leads for future listings. Agents who never hold open houses lose out on much fun with people and also on opportunities for new business. That held true years ago and still is true today. That will never change.

I usually had a guest list at an open house and asked people to sign in when they arrived. A seller will also appreciate a guest list, so they know who came into their home. This list can give you phone numbers, addresses and e-mail addresses in addition to names to follow up on, if you make a space for all of that information.

As I said, people will decide within a few minutes if they like a house or not. Tests have been made that showed people make a positive or negative decision within the first three minutes of entering a house. Therefore, it is of the utmost importance to help a seller stage the home. That means asking them to clean the property up completely. It has to be spotless, inside and out. If there is a lot of clutter, ask the owner to remove the clutter and leave only a few key pieces of decoration and furniture in place. Often I asked them to box up what they did not need during the selling process and store these things away. This practice makes moving later much easier, as much is boxed up already.

A house will look much larger and more open without clutter. Space is a luxury everyone appreciates. Clean windows add sparkle. Yards should be well kept, and the grass should be mowed. Sometimes it takes a little work to convince a seller that these things need to be done, but when I told them they would realize a higher price for their home if they followed my advice, they usually went along with the program. At the end of showings or open houses I would give them a report, either in writing or verbally, to let them know how they went. It is important to keep the client informed and also to call them and give them updates about the progress.

As I mentioned before, staying in touch with the client is a key to success in real estate. If you don't do that, the client will assume, rightfully, that you have no interest in the sale and that you don't care. Your client will eventually drop you and hire another agent. That is not what you want to happen after you invested much time and many advertising dollars into the listing.

Usually women buyers look at kitchens and bathrooms, male buyers at the garage and the basement. Kitchens have to be inviting and clean, as do the bathrooms. Dirty sinks and toilets and stained tubs are a turnoff. If you replace fixtures that are unsightly and old, you are ahead of the game and will get your investment back, plus higher profits, and at the same time improve the chances of a faster sale.

I am always amazed when people place their property on the market and hope for a great price without making the smallest improvements or even keeping it clean! A house should at least be clean, if nothing else. You should always advise your sellers and insist on cleanings, tidying up, and removing trash and clutter if you hope to make a sale on that property.

If a seller refuses to clean up a property and it is offensive, don't take the listing. It will be wasted time for you, and chances for a sale are very slim.

CHAPTER 8

Becoming an investor/builder

Another lucrative way to make mullah in real estate is to build homes, of course. No one is born a contractor; you become one after investing time and learning the building trade. Obviously you will need a valid contractor's license to build homes, and you will need to pass tests to obtain your license. A contractor needs to submit his or her building plans to the county's or city's (depending on location) building department for inspection to pass building codes for every aspect of the construction; that is, general design, foundation, plumbing, electrical, water supply, grading of the property, etc. At various phases of the construction, the contractor will call the building inspector to come and sign off on that particular phase of the construction. This procedure ensures that no problems creep up later and reduces the possibility that work might need to be redone at great expense.

Never make a major renovation or consider new construction without observing the existing building codes and having a county building inspector sign off on the work. The codes exist for a very good reason, and every legitimate contractor is keenly aware of them. Building permits and inspections are not costly compared to making major mistakes and having to pay for the corrected work later.

If you consider making renovations that include changing some electrical or plumbing work in a house, always "pull a permit" and have the work re-inspected when it is completed.

The Charlie story

Here is an example of how you can be successful as an investor/agent while teaming up with a contractor.

I had met "Charlie" while he was doing some work on my own house in California. I was very impressed with his skills and expertise as a carpenter, his overall knowledge of plumbing and electrical work, and the speed with which he accomplished the project. One day I asked him if he would be interested in building a house with me as his financial partner and agent who would place the house on the market and sell it once it was completed. I would find the lot and purchase it and obtain a construction loan. Charlie's finances were in poor shape, but he was a gifted contractor. To my delight he agreed to my plan.

He would do the construction; I would find the lot, get the construction loan, and sell the finished property. We would split the gain between us. It was the perfect partnership, and we formed an LLC, a limited liability corporation, with all duties and obligations of each partner clearly spelled out.

I went right to work and purchased a wonderful property with a 30 percent down payment on a lagoon in California with beautiful views, in a quiet location. Charlie applied for and received the building permits for his plans for the house construction he had drawn up, with some modifications. I loved his design for a great room in the main living area, a fireplace and super-modern kitchen, high ceilings, fabulous baths, and a two-car garage under the house you could drive into from the road. This was a big plus, as many houses in California don't have garages; they are built into the hills on wooden support beams. Our house also had a large deck overlooking the lagoon.

Once his work was completed—and it took many months with the construction materials purchased from timely bank payouts of the construction loan—I put the house on the market. I had staged it and started my open houses and advertisements. I sold it pretty fast to a young couple with a disclosed dual agency, as they did not have an agent, so I had a double commission as well. We had invested about $300,000 in total and sold it for $640,000, and after paying off the loans (not much cash had been invested) we split the proceeds between us, which amounted to $170,000 each. This was a very nice gain, which we had to pay capital gains tax on, of course. But it was still well worth the amount of work that went into the project for both of us.

When later on I moved to Florida with my husband, I hoped that Charlie might move down there as well, so we could do another project. To my delight he actually agreed and started his move cross-country with his trailer and dog, but he was "waylaid by a redhead" in New Orleans, as he told me on the phone, and I never saw him again.

However, this story is an example of what you might be able to do as an agent if you know a good, licensed, and knowledgeable contractor who is willing to team up with you. Or, should the reader be a contractor, perhaps you could find an agent or broker who has the finances you might not have at the moment and form a partnership with him or her for gain.

CHAPTER 9

Working as a buyer's agent

Advice #1. Ask for proof of funds.

When you are a buyer's agent, always, always ask for proof of funds before you set out to show properties to the buyer. This person or persons expect you to spend your valuable time with them to show and drive them around. You have a right to ask them to show you that they are able to buy. Some people make it their Sunday excursion to look at properties, when in fact they don't have the money or the ability to buy anything at all. To establish that prospective buyers have funds, I always asked new clients to meet me at the office, we sat down in the conference room, and we went over their desires and plans. This discussion *always* included asking them to show me that they had the funds to accomplish their goal. If they did not show up for that meeting or were hazy about their funds or did not want to discuss this valuable point, I knew I had wasted the time of only one scheduled meeting, not hours and hours of driving them around and showing them houses they could or would never buy.

Advice #2. Prequalification.

Have your buyer get prequalified for a loan with a lender of his or her choice. You can recommend three or more mortgage brokers and banks, but leave the choice to the buyer. You can never accept a fee kickback from a friendly lender; it is not allowed. I have seen some agents go out and show houses for days only to discover that their clients could not afford to buy. A lender will check their credit on the spot. Don't waste your time with a buyer who does not bring a prequalification letter or bank approval letter back to you within a few days, no matter how anxious you are to make a sale. They will appreciate your professionalism. Some real estate companies have a mortgage broker in their office; you can refer your clients to that broker or to others.

Advice #3. Working with a buyer to purchase from a developer.

Always list your name and broker's office plus the client's name with the developer before sitting down with the developer's sales agent in their office. If you don't protect yourself that way, you have no proof that you brought this buyer to the development and you may never see a commission.

A Florida developer story

There was a company in Florida that was very successful. The person with the most sales in the office would tell any customer you brought as their agent, "I only have one more of these homes available; the rest are sold out." She was telling your client that he or she had better buy today, or there would be no more homes available like the one your buyer liked. There were a few sold signs on the lots, strategically placed around the development, when in fact dozens more of the same model would be built and were already planned for construction, which both she and I knew very well. I told my client in private that I believed more houses would be built just like the one he had chosen, but he wanted to go ahead anyway.

The buyer had very little money to put down, only 3 percent, and that was borrowed, which is entirely against the rules. Down payments have to be made from available funds and cannot be borrowed, as I explained previously. At that time the down payment funds needed to be in the buyer's account for at least ninety days before the closing, actually quite a short period of time. (Different lenders have different rules at this time.) The lender stood to make a fortune over the time of the loan. The developer was also the lender, which is often the case.

The risk was small for the lender, as the borrower, my client, was a professional, well-educated man and would in all probability keep making the payments. Everyone won; however, the buyer would now pay three to four times the loan amount back to the lender over the time of the loan, and he had huge up-front penalty fees for the small down payment. I explained all this to my client, but his decision was to go ahead with the purchase anyway, as he needed a house for his family. It was a good deal for everyone, especially for the lender/developer, who was also funding the loan, and as the builder, he was also rid of another house on his lots. We agents were paid 5 percent together to be split on the sale price of the home. That is standard real estate practice; however, some developers may pay a 6 percent commission on the sale price. My client now owned a home he and his family loved and would enjoy living in—a good ending to this story.

Bad lending practices from banks story

A friend of mine, a sweet younger woman, completely innocent about purchasing a home, and financing, and other real estate matters, was talked into buying a one-bedroom condo by an unscrupulous agent. She could not afford it at all. My friend had rented a cottage from me, and the rent was low; however, she had trouble making these low payments each month. She was a server in a restaurant and occasionally did facials when she had a client; not much money was coming in and even then sporadically at best. I told her not to buy, as she could not afford it. I could not bring myself to sell her anything, as I liked her as a human being. She was a truly nice and gentle person. When one day she told me that she had found a one-bedroom apartment she wanted to buy, she asked me to have a look at it. I consented, but with trepidation.

The apartment needed a lot of work—a new kitchen, new baths, flooring, etc. It was a mess, but the other agent told her it was "a good deal." Nothing I said could persuade my friend not to go forward with the purchase.

I asked her if I could come to the closing and to allow me to look at her loan documents and purchase agreement. I told her that she could walk away even at closing and did not have to go through with the deal. When everyone was assembled at the conference table in the title company's office, I asked to look at the papers. I was horrified. I knew she had no money to put down. She had borrowed the down payment from her credit cards, a big mistake, but again conveniently overlooked by the mortgage broker, who charged her three points (3 percent) up front for his services. One of the basic rules in real estate is to never purchase any property with a borrowed down payment, as I have mentioned now several times. The 3 percent interest, or points charge the mortgage broker took was built into the loan, and she had to pay interest on that for the next thirty years. In addition, she had to pay interest on the borrowed down payment, plus making the mortgage payment, the home owner association fee payment, and property taxes. She could not support these payments with her income.

The loan itself was at an interest rate of 9 percent, a usury interest rate even at that time, because of her bad credit history. When someone's credit is marginal or bad, the interest rate is jacked up, a practice by the lenders as an excuse to make increased profits for the "risk" they are taking. This is a standard banking practice. They should have just denied the loan, which gratefully they now do after the 2008 fiasco. But in my friend's case they unfortunately approved the loan.

My poor friend now had a huge monthly payment to make to live in a place that still needed a ton of work. She somehow was able to get some more funds from her credit cards to remodel the kitchen and bath ... more to pay every month she could not afford. Do I have to tell you this story has a bad ending? When I saw the closing documents, I advised her to walk away from the deal, but she said to me she "wanted the condo," and she signed on the bottom line! She was now in deep trouble.

The real estate agents had made $6,250 (5 percent) to be split two ways, the mortgage broker had made another $3,750 on the loan, the lender had also charged $3,750 up front on the loan, and my poor friend would pay approximately $437,500 over thirty years for a $125,000 purchase of a small condo that needed much work. All the fees everyone was making, except for the commissions, which the seller paid, had been incorporated into the loan, a standard practice. She now had to pay off her credit cards for a long, long time; her credit history was even worse than before; plus she would be making the large mortgage payments. A very bad ending! The banks are at fault for giving such loans to people like my friend. It was unconscionable, and these tactics were a huge part of the banking breakdown.

"New buyer in town" story

A young woman contacted me about wanting to purchase a home in the area. She had transferred from another state and was unfamiliar with the area. I had been recommended and was happy to help her and show her areas that were safe and affordable for her. She did not like anything I showed her, and she wanted a "good deal." She felt I had not shown her everything that was available. She even asked why I did not show her all that was available, but I had no reason not to do so.

However, I thought that she did not trust me and stopped calling her; some buyers feel they know better than the expert, and I let it go. One day she called and told me (I guess to rub it in) that she had bought a condo in an area I had "withheld" from her. I asked what that area was. And I was amazed again: another agent had sold her a place in a run-down part of town, which was not well managed and not kept up. *There was a bit of "steering" involved here*, I thought to myself. Steering is when agents recommend that people buy in a certain area and keep them out of others; it is unethical and punishable by law. The buyer was from another part of the world; she was well educated and was going to work for a large company in that area of Florida. Her agent had made her commission, but this educated and smart woman was now living in a less than desirable area with values declining steadily. She would have a loss if she ever wanted to sell again. Properties moved very slowly there and stayed on the market for a long time. An unscrupulous agent? Well, heck, yes, and it is happening all the time.

Agents make their living by making commissions, and obviously without a sale there is no commission. Some agents are driven by greed or a fundamental need to make a living, and they have influenced millions of buyers in the country over time to make poor or even bad decisions when buying property, just because they needed to pay that month's bills. Understandable? Yes! Justified? No! Don't become one of those agents.

CHAPTER 10

Working as a listing or sales agent

Choose your listings carefully

The sheep story

One day I received a call from a South American home owner living in one of the small towns of Northern California. He wanted to put his house on the market to buy something larger for his family with several children. The house was older with a few bedrooms and a small yard in the back. It was all fenced in, which is always good for people with kids or pets. It seemed a nice place to sell. The property had a good address with excellent schools around and was located in a coveted area. It was simple, but in that town anything could be sold. The owner and I met; the wife was nowhere to be seen. He proceeded to show me around the property. It all looked fine, and I was thinking about pricing. I had done some research before getting there, as I always liked to be prepared.

When we came to the kitchen, I had a nasty surprise. There was a pot on the stove with a skull in it and large eyes glaring at me. I let out a scream and fled from the kitchen. The wife was cooking a sheep's head and had not covered the pot. I excused myself and left the house without further conversations. I did not want the listing. If the owners cook a sheep's head when an agent comes to the house, I could not take a risk and have showings with possibly such a horrible sight in the kitchen again. It was not worth the trouble and time, and I did not want to deal with it. Had I told them that it was not acceptable to me, they would not have understood. "Different strokes for different folks."

A Halloween Story

Another time I received a phone call from a potential seller who lived in a home in the area I "farmed" and lived in. He had read the "Sold Neighborhood Report" I had mailed out earlier, and he wanted to meet with me. He was thinking about selling his home and wanted my input on pricing. As was my custom, I first did a drive-by of his property to determine if I wanted to meet with him and also to find out what the location was all about. The house was situated on a hilly road leading to the entry of a country club, a good location. So we arranged for a meeting at the property. I did my usual research and printed out various "sold" and various "on active market" homes to show him. I normally would then do a walk-through of the home after a discussion with the owner and find out what his goals and thoughts were and what price he hoped to realize.

Most often sellers have a pretty good idea what they want for their home and have done some of their own research. But often sellers have unrealistic ideas about their values, and sometimes they rely entirely on the suggestion of the agent. Relying on the suggestion of the agent could be a bad mistake on their part, if they contracted with an agent who was looking for a fast buck. Underpricing a property will lead to a faster sale, of course, and therefore to a faster commission.

So we met, and the seller was a single man. The house at first impression looked very nice and very saleable on a good lot, though with a drop-off in the back of the property, but that was often the case in California. It was nicely furnished and showed well.

But then I noticed that strange items peeked out from under some of the furniture—an arm here, stuffed but very realistic, a shoe and sock there, and a hand lying under a table … in different rooms of the house.

I asked him what these items were and why he had placed them there; it was a shock at first to see them, as it was *not* Halloween, not even close to Halloween. He smiled and said he enjoyed seeing visitors perplexed or shocked like me. I asked him if he would remove these items for the sale, and he simply said, "No." This person was obviously somewhat disturbed, and I quickly said my good-bye and left, having absolutely no interest in selling his property, no matter what the commission would have been. It takes all types, but this was a type I did not want to deal with.

Unrealistic sellers story

A couple I knew met with me at their home and said they were thinking about placing their house on the market. I had done my usual research about property values in their neighborhood in Florida, and after looking around I knew it as worth what the other houses near them had

©Lynette Yencho

sold for. The figure was about half a million dollars. When I suggested that sales price, they were very annoyed and said they would not sell for less than a million dollars. That price was completely unrealistic, and I thanked them for their time and said my good-byes.

There was no point in taking that listing. Some agents will accept such an overpriced listing in the hope that eventually they can wear the owners down to a lower price point. That may be the case with a smaller spread between the seller's expectations and the agent's true assessment of a home, but when you are talking about half a million dollars, that gap cannot be closed. So be careful as an agent where you want to spend your time and money! A property listing that sits on the market for years because the price is much too high will get old and stale, and other agents will no longer show it.

General advice about selling a property

An excellent way to sell a house is to point out all the positive and interesting features. You should note these features on a property detail sales sheet, which should be placed in any home that is for sale by a Realtor. Unfortunately agents often will not do so, a mistake on their part, as visitors will often take the sheet with them and may call the agent later for another sale or purchase.

Even improvement possibilities should be mentioned if the house needs work. Sell a vision of the future—what the property could be like, what it could become. If you are hired by a seller, open up a Pandora's Box of possibilities and a buyer will often buy a fantasy, features that are not yet visible. We all like the dream of the perfect home, don't we?

This has been a successful method of selling for me quite often. You have seen the words *room for a pool*, and even if the pool is never built, at least the possibility is there for one, and that leaves the buyer with a sense of anticipation for what might be. And there is nothing wrong with that. Often a buyer may not possess the vision for what could be done with a house or garden and may appreciate some suggestions for improvements.

The suggestion for an improved kitchen with granite countertops or the expansion of a room into a sunroom overlooking a garden might not have occurred to the buyer. And he or she is getting your advice for free and doesn't have to pay an interior decorator for it.

Of course, you need to assess your customers carefully. If they are people with definite ideas of their own and deep pockets to pay for professional help, it is best to step aside and simply perform your agent's functions ... process the documents, do the negotiations necessary, and help close escrow efficiently.

Presenting a purchase offer to a seller's agent story

Often listing agents will receive their own offer for a property they market for the seller. And that is perfectly fine; they can work as a dual agent as long as buyer and seller are all right with it and it is disclosed to both. This relationship is disclosed on a form all parties must sign. Today you call it being a "transaction broker." The form everyone signs is the agency disclosure; it is required on all transactions.

However, if you bring in an offer for a property as a buyer's agent for your own buyer, you should always ask if any other offers are on the table. It is also best not to alert listing agents that you are working on an offer, as they may escalate their efforts to write up their own offer from an interested party they may have been working with, and they may beat you to the punch with the sellers. You should certainly *never* tell a listing agent what kind of offer you have or for how much before you submit it. Today, most offers are submitted electronically via the Internet to the listing agent; so you are not fully protected, as you cannot present the offer to the seller yourself anymore, as we used to do. That was a huge advantage at the time.

Listing agents now have full power over wheeling and dealing with offers. Why should you be careful? Well, it is obvious: if the listing agent makes the sale, he or she will get a double commission. If a buyer's agent brings in the offer, he or she will receive only 50 percent of the 5 or 6 percent commission on the sale price.

I myself brought an offer recently on a property in California at a higher price than the seller received in the end, because the listing agent was playing games with the offers. I had offered $185,000 in a very competitive market with multiple offers and was told the seller refused my offer. The property was listed at $165,000. I had offered $20,000 more than the asking price! When I later checked the "sold price" (easily available on Trulia. com or Realtor.com), I found it had been sold for $165,000, with the listing agent receiving a 6 percent commission. Was there anything I could do about it? No, not really.

This is the game of real estate. Sometimes you win, and sometimes you lose. But not all agents are dishonest; for the most part they are honest and truly want to receive the best price for the client's property, which in fact is their duty. Be one of the honest agents!

Therefore, as a buyer or as a seller, it is best to work with an agent who is recommended with testimonials and phone numbers you can call for references, and one who has been in business for many years.

When you interview agents for a sale or a purchase of your property, ask for phone numbers and references. As an agent, have such a list available when you get interviewed. It creates confidence in your possible client.

CHAPTER 11

Negotiation skills—don't stop the action in midstream

The ability to negotiate is a crucial skill if you want to be a successful agent. You can develop this skill, just as I did; I was not born with it. Negotiations are where most contracts fall apart if they are not handled correctly.

Many agents make a fundamental mistake when presenting an offer to purchase from their buyer to a seller. Some buyers test the seller by making a lowball offer, when they are perfectly willing and able to pay a higher price. They just want to see if the seller might accept their low offer, and sometimes they may get lucky and the seller will accept the low price. If the offer is way below the belt, the seller may refuse to deal with it and may want to throw the offer into the trash.

Always encourage your clients to keep the ball rolling. Encourage the seller to write up a counteroffer even if he or she is annoyed. The buyer just may come up in price and purchase the property. Perhaps he or she was just testing the waters. Counteroffers should always be written and may just save the deal and your commission. If the counteroffer fails, write a counter to the counter; all parts might just fall into place for an acceptance of the offer.

I saw too many deals fall by the wayside over the years because they were mishandled by agents who did not even attempt to negotiate the deal. Sometimes emotional barriers or hurdles need to be overcome. A good agent will know how to handle that. An agent has to be a bit of a psychologist at times. Just letting a sale go and leaving all parties frustrated is not good for your reputation either. Even if you never meet the seller, you can find out from his or her agent what the problem might be and perhaps overcome it by counseling your client accordingly. Letting an escrow fail when issues could have been remedied is not a situation you want to happen in your professional career. This is also good advice to sellers of a property. An offer they let go might have been the best offer they ever received in the end.

CHAPTER 12

Losses of 2008 and an auction story

I had listed my own properties for sale with the company I was working with. I wanted to sell them again, all four of them, after I obtained my Florida license. Well, that was in 2006, and in 2008 the market collapsed, as we all know. The rules have changed forever. Had I accepted the pricing of 2006 then, I would be a happier person now. But I held out for a higher price, and that higher price never came; instead, values were dropping steadily. No one foresaw the events that unfolded, though there had been warnings about the possible collapse of the real estate bubble. No one was paying attention to it, as far as I knew, except for a few wise and very lucky people.

Auction today!

©Lynette Yencho

As one of my properties was now costing me more than it brought in as a rental, it made sense to sell it quickly. I contacted an auction house my real estate company was connected with and listed the property with them to be auctioned off. It did not sell at auction either, and the values were still falling. So I rented it out again.

However, one good thing that came out this auction effort was that I received a call from someone out of state who was interested in purchasing another auction listing for over $4 million. I worked with this buyer for several weeks and kept him on track, sent e-mails and made phone calls to the buyer, and sent brochures and info on the property he himself requested from me. That property also had not sold at an auction. In the end the buyer purchased this lovely estate after several weeks of negotiation.

However, before closing the buyer and seller got together in private and reduced the sales commissions between themselves from the usual about 5 percent to 3 percent overall between all agents. Obviously that made a huge financial difference at that price point. I had personally shown the buyer the property and introduced him to the seller (a big mistake!) at the buyer's insistence, something I normally never do! But the buyer felt in the end that my recommendation was warranted, and he bought the estate.

Suddenly, just before the closing, I received a phone call from an agent in the same office, someone I had never heard of before. He claimed that he was entitled to my commission. This person did not know my buyer, nor had he ever heard of him.

Two years prior, he had introduced the seller to the auctioneers, who had no listing agreement. The agent didn't have one either. The phone call was his only involvement. To my amazement and total consternation, my broker awarded this agent a large commission and shorted mine by 40 percent. To get paid at all, I had to agree in writing to never sue the brokerage. It turned out that the other agent was one of their "pet agents," as we say in the business.

Needless to say, I left the company and took my business elsewhere. The auctioneers also disassociated themselves from this broker and were never heard from again. They had to sign similar disclosures to receive their severely cut commissions, as well. My own commission was reduced by the agreement between buyer and seller to only 3 percent overall; on top of that, a huge part was given to another agent for an "introduction." I had brought the buyer; without that important factor there would have been *no* sale!

The moral of this story for agents?

1. 1. Never introduce buyers and sellers before the closing if you can avoid it.
2. 2. Work for an honest broker; speak to the agents working there to find out whether they are happy with their broker.

Selling a friend's home? You may lose a friend story

Whenever I took a listing in my long career, I tried my best to get the seller the best and the highest price. That used to be the guideline of every honest and hardworking agent. Today that may no longer be the case, as prices are all over the map with the many foreclosures and short sales now. However, with the market improving again over the ever-falling prices after 2008 and 2009, Realtors have a good chance today to sell homes at a fair market value. In some areas like Manhattan and Miami, San Francisco and San Diego, however, properties are now selling at record prices to buyers from China, South America, and Russia.

One three-story apartment in a New York skyscraper recently sold for over $100 million.

In Florida some friends contacted me to sell their condo by the beach. I accepted, though I knew that their asking price was unrealistic. I did not want to bring the bad news to them too early, but I knew from comps (comparative selling property prices in the same neighborhood within the last six months, as I said before) what the actual selling price probably would be. My friends would tell me, "But it's close to the beach, just a few steps away, and we remodeled the kitchen, etc."

In any market all these factors may have some importance, but most of all, markets are always price driven. The other important factor is to find the one buyer who is willing and able to buy and get a loan, or has cash to buy with. I was lucky and brought a buyer to my friends with cash, and she who also liked the condo … whew! She was a young woman, single and a beach lover. But she offered less than asking price. My friends did not want to accept. After working the listing for several months with showings, open houses, meetings with the sellers, and all the other work involved, I finally was able to explain that the market would not get better at any time soon due to our economy, but was steadily worsening at that time. I feared that later on the condo would bring even less than the offer I had received, and history proved me right. The same type of condos are now selling for much less indeed.

At last my friends accepted after countering the offer, and we closed the deal. The sad part to this story is that I hardly ever heard from my friends again. I believe they still think that I did not get them what the condo was worth. They were also convinced that their home was worth over a million, when in fact it was worth maybe $400,000 at the time.

It is tough to please everyone and tougher to lose a friend when in fact you had actually helped them. But I had helped a young woman into a nice condo she loved.

Margot, the millionaire beggar story

She was a German woman I had helped in California, while I was living and working there as a Realtor.

This unusual woman was twelve years older than I, which made her sixteen years old when the Russians marched into Germany ... a bad time. She had a sister of about the same age. To forget the war years and to get away from their awful memories, they both immigrated to the States and married American men in due time. Both were blond and pretty when young. They lived on the same street but did not speak with each other anymore when I knew Margot. At around age forty she suffered a stroke that left her totally paralyzed on the right side; she dragged her right leg and was always holding her limp, useless right arm with her left hand. Her husband had died eight years earlier, after taking care of her for many years.

After the stroke Margot lost her knowledge of English due to an impediment in her brain and could speak and think only in German. Since I was German born and a German-speaking Realtor, I was able to help her with the sale of a property. The house she lived in was neglected, and there were boxes and trays on her kitchen table in which she had brought food home from the county's senior food program weeks earlier. The backyard of her house was a jungle.

When I spoke with Margot in German, she was lucid and knew exactly what she wanted. She was living on a very small Social Security check and had no money. She was seventy-two years old when I met her and had been living half-paralyzed for thirty years. None of her American family members from her sister's side was helping her with her disability.

At the senior food program the people thought of her as the crazy German woman. And they all thought she was poor, when in fact she was worth about one and a half million dollars. She was a millionaire, not in cash (as she had none) or securities, but in property values.

Margot had plenty of American family members, her sister's offspring, who had all abandoned her in hopes of her dying sooner rather than later, so they could inherit her money. One day I brought my cleaning ladies to Margot's house and, under her screams of protest, the two nice women gathered up large sacks of debris and garbage and hauled them out to their van to take away. But Margot hobbled outside and dragged two of the bags back inside and riffled through them, but finding only more plastic bags, containers, and garbage. She placed them back into the mother's bedroom with her mother's ashes.

Margot knew that I was helping her as a friend. I did not need the commission. I had worked hard and long hours to become of one of the most successful Realtors in the county. My interest in helping her went deeply into the subconscious and connected with memories of what I had lived through as a four-year-old child in Berlin when Russian soldiers had invaded my home. I wanted to help Margot and change her life into a comfortable one she could easily afford, once I sold her investment property. The house she lived in was mortgage free. All she had to do was to keep paying her property taxes, which she had managed to do over the years, but she had not made any repairs to the house whatsoever.

So I went to work selling her triplex, which she had built together with her deceased husband twenty-five years earlier. This triplex had stayed vacant since it had been built. It was sitting at a busy intersection in a great small town, but its only desirable attribute was the location, because of its terrible condition.

I put it on the market for just under a million. Inside the building was full of mold. The apartments had been vandalized, rain had gotten into the doors and windows, the carpets were foul, and the appliances were all rusted out. I advertised this almost unsalable property, and a miracle happened. Someone offered a good price, and the buyer knew he had to take the building down to the studs and entirely rebuild it and perform a complete mold remediation.

I brought the offer to Margot, and after a long struggle with her (she also had unrealistic ideas about the value of this property), she finally accepted the offer and signed the documents. Had this property been sold today, it would never have brought the price anymore—perhaps only half of that.

After closing the escrow, when I took her the big check from the escrow company, we were both very excited and happy. I accompanied her to a large bank and helped her open an investment account with only herself as the signatory on it and none of her family members. Of course she had to pay substantial taxes to Uncle Sam.

Margot was a fairly rich woman now, and she finally could let go of the burden she had lived with for twenty-five years. She had owned a property that could not be rented due to its condition and her inability to deal with tenants due to her stroke and lack of English. It had brought her no income for twenty-five years, just expenses. It was very close to being taken by the county. Margot had not paid her property taxes for several years. That auction day was closer than Margot liked to believe; it was only a month away when the escrow closed.

I often think of my friend Margot, and I have called her on different occasions. She always has been happy to hear from me, her friend. She always says she will visit me soon ...

The drug bust story

Another Realtor I know had rented one of his properties to a young unmarried couple. They looked clean, and the young woman was very pretty. Both were very well dressed. They wanted to rent his house in a private gated community for about a year. He thought, *Okay, why not?* It seemed reasonable enough. They told him that they also owned a single-family home about half an hour away in a non-gated, more rural area of Florida, which they eventually showed to him.

The house was not occupied and was still furnished, sitting vacant. They said they just did not want to live there anymore and wanted to be in a gated community for security reasons. The property bordered on a runoff canal like thousands in Florida, with undeveloped land behind it, full of brush and palms and palmettos for miles. There was no fence in the back of the

©Lynette Yencho

property, just in front of the house with an electronic gate and along the sides of it. There was plenty of wildlife in this area, including alligators from the canal, as well as snakes and other animals.

Behind the house was also a large, sturdy metal shed with triple locks, and lighting and fans inside. They called it their hurricane shelter, but my friend suspected it could have been a place where they dried marijuana, which could have been growing on the other side of the canal. It was none of his business and he did not ask—did not care what they did with the shed. The young man owned plenty of toys, including several motorcycles, lawn mowers, and a speedboat sitting under another open shed; he drove a BMW and had other toys. It seemed he was unemployed but had plenty of cash. He never missed a rent payment and always paid the rent in cash.

Both tenants seemed to enjoy my friend's house and the fact that it was on a golf course and well maintained by him. The young man bought a golf cart and stored it in the garage along with the two other cars they owned. One day he asked if he could buy the house. My friend was willing to sell for the right price, and they agreed to the sale with a contract. Then he asked my Realtor friend to sell his house in the rural area to raise the funds for the purchase in cash. He listed the property and worked with both of them to get the house ready for the sale. It was not going to be an easy sale. The house was a wooden structure with just a concrete perimeter foundation underneath, and no basement. Of course, virtually no houses in Florida have basements; everything is built with slabs, basically on sand. The main living area was on the second floor, with a larger (master) bedroom on the third floor and only a second bedroom on the main level. From the living area one had a good view of anyone coming to the house; there would be no surprise visitors coming through the front gate, and certainly no one would come from the jungle in the back.

The facts that the house had only two bedrooms instead of the usually preferred three, was made of wood instead of concrete, and had lots of steps inside were three detrimental attributes for a sale. My friend told his clients about the problems, and they understood. After several months and some showings he finally received an acceptable offer. There had been one or two other unacceptable ones previously.

The clients were excited, as they truly wanted to purchase his rental property and were now getting close. Documents were drawn up and signed, the buyers' loan was approved, the survey was made, and the appraisal came in at the sale price. It all looked very good, and my friend had spent many weeks on this deal, including staging their old house for the sale. The young couple, the sellers, would be happy—they would have sold their house to the new buyer—and my friend would close on their purchase of his own property the same day after many weeks of work.

It was a win-win situation for everyone. But on the very morning of the closing my agent friend received a phone call from the other agent representing the new buyer for his tenant's old house. His client had been arrested for selling drugs and was in jail; there would be no closing, ever!

My friend's tenants/buyers moved out of his rental property and moved back into their old house. They broke the lease and the purchase contract, and he had to find a new tenant. There are times when real estate can be a real problem and a headache. But there are always better times ahead!

CHAPTER 13

Thinking about selling your house your-
self without real estate experience?

Selling a house yourself without real estate experience is not something I would recommend doing. But often sellers think about the thousands of dollars they could save if they sold on their own. And that is definitely appealing. However, not being familiar with the selling process and the real estate business could lead into a labyrinth of problems, with greater losses at the end, than if you allow an agent to handle the sale for you in a professional way and pay the commission.

Pitfalls could include underpricing the house and leaving money on the table or overpricing it and not selling at all—just wasting time. A professional agent will be able to help set the correct price for your property and market it; today's Internet and electronic market use many different channels giving you a much wider audience, market, and exposure. If you believe that you can sell your home to someone who just happens to drive by and see your For Sale sign, you are probably mistaken. Research shows that less than 2 percent of all for-sale-by-owner sales succeed. Advertising your own home is also quite expensive, and there is the risk of showing your home to people who are not in the market to purchase at all, just snooping around or out for a Sunday drive and entertainment.

Professional agents will determine the background of interested parties, asking for financial information to ascertain that they are able to purchase and are not wasting the agent's time. They will ask for financial statements at the first meeting before they will show a client around (at least a seasoned agent will do so, whereas a novice agent might storm off with clients without obtaining the necessary background information). They will bring a client to your property only when they believe that the client is in a financial position to buy.

If you, as the owner, ask the interested party to show you bank statements, you might feel embarrassed to do so, or worse, the person you ask might simply refuse to reveal such personal information to you. You would have no way of knowing whom you are dealing with. A professional agent will then, upon receipt of an offer, do all the paperwork for you ... and that is a lot of work today. There are many disclosures, and dealings with mortgage brokers, appraisers, banks, surveyors, inspectors, etc. As a private person you have no way of knowing how to handle all that, and it is getting more complicated all the time, with more disclosures required by law, the state, the local authorities, and attorneys.

Having an agent represent your interests is money well spent and can actually save you thousands of dollars in the long run. An agent can negotiate for you should problems arise during the escrow process. The agent will look at all disclosures and make sure they are understood and signed by all parties; he or she will lead you through the escrow and closing process and make sure that all dots are there and all documentation is handled in a timely fashion.

Agents will keep a transaction calendar and make sure all parties stay within the contract; that way, no one can flake out or change their mind in midstream because a signature was forgotten somewhere. Such mistakes can leave the door open for the buyer to walk away on a pretense because he or she had a change of heart or buyer's remorse, as happens often. Usually these obstacles are overcome by efficient agents, justifying any commission paid to them. Good agents will keep the escrow flowing expertly and close your sale or purchase in a timely manner. This is the most difficult part of being an agent, and that is where most home owners who sell a property by themselves will undoubtedly fail most of the time. If you are a former agent, however, your knowledge may lead you to possible success.

Should you insist on selling a property yourself, you may want to check out websites such as ForSalebyOwner.com, Housepad. com, and others (research them on Google), which will list your property online with the MLS for a one-time fee of $495. They will e-mail you all the forms you need to place your property on the local MLS. Each state requires that listings be placed on the Multiple Listing Service by a broker who is licensed in that state. There are brokers today who have licenses in various states and do nothing but keep them current. They charge home owners a simple fee of about $495 and place your listing on the MLS for you. Other agents will see the new listing and call the seller to show the property to their buyer.

Obviously you have to be available for these showings, and of course you will need to accommodate them to sell your property and pay the buyer's agent commission of 2.5 to 3 percent. If you offer to pay less, your chances of selling are vastly diminished; agents usually don't show any property unless they receive at least a 2.5 percent commission, as they have to split that with their brokers. All commissions are prearranged and appear on the listing of the property. Listings without a commission percentage will be taken off the Multiple Listing Service to protect the agents and brokers.

For Sale by Owner success story

How I saved a commission payment by working with Housepad.com

I recently bought a foreclosure property in Kansas City for $62,000, put about $15,000 in renovation costs into it, and sold it after the remodel for $126,000. I paid only the buyer's agent commission of 2.5 percent and saved the listing agent's commission of the usual 2.5 percent by listing it myself with Housepad. com. The broker was in another state altogether but was licensed in Missouri and many other states of the Union, as well. The listing commission cost me $495, not 2.5 percent, or $3,150. A nice savings. Housepad.com will e-mail you all the forms you need, such as seller's disclosures, which are required from any seller, and the lead-based paint disclosures, which are required by law. The agent representing the buyer will supply the sales contract for you. You can also call Housepad.com with any questions you may have. Should you sell your property yourself to a buyer, they will e-mail you a sales contract, as well.

But if you are totally inexperienced in real estate, this path may not be right for you; you would be better off with an agent to list your property to avoid pitfalls and possible later lawsuits.

FORECLOSURE

©Lynette Yencho

CHAPTER 14

Shopping for a listing/seller's agent

What to do and not to do when selecting a real estate agent to sell your house

First of all, you need to know that there are several types of agents. I will describe each type to you in the following sequence, and of course some cross the lines from one into another. But they all have certain characteristics, which I will attempt to tell you about.

1. *The old battle-axes:* These are usually women, and usually they have been around a long time—twenty years or more. They no longer dress sharply, as they don't give a hoot anymore, and they spend a lot of time with other agents in the office chatting. They know the ropes, but their energy has slowed, and they will take certain short-cuts and try to get it done for less. They are always in the office, and they tend to complain a lot. Only big sales will get them excited.

2. *The listing collectors:* These people, sometimes women, sometimes men, usually dress sharply. Their business is show business. They can speak with a golden tongue.

Their modus operandi is to collect listings, and they run the largest ads in the papers, sometimes whole pages filled with photos of themselves and properties they have listed, will list, or have sold (some a long time ago). Their ego is larger than the splashy car they drive to impress you, the seller. They will come into your home, walk around with confidence, and take the listing, and that is the last time you will see them. They will now turn over the listing to their assistants, who are usually newly hired people with a license but no experience at all. They will work for the ego man or woman for a salary. Whenever you call your agent from now on, you will get the assistant. The listing taker has done his or her job—taking the listing. He or she will now sit back and wait for another agent to sell the property. The assistant will place the ads, take the calls, show the property, and hold open houses. I know of some such agents who never, ever held an open house.

I know of one very successful listing taker who made his fortune with a simple trick. He placed beautiful flower arrangements in the homes he listed. These flowers were brought in by professional florists by the truckloads at great cost and then were taken away again after the photo shooting session. The listings looked fabulous in real estate magazines and online photos, and it worked for him. He was a man with a very large ego and rarely spoke to other agents. His income was higher than that of the president of the United States, higher by far, and he was very impressed with himself. Since all his listings were in the $2 million to $7 million range, it did not take a lot of sales to make that kind of money.

3. *The obsessive working agent:* This is the agent who will work day and night, all week long, and this is the favorite agent of any real estate company. They work themselves

into a frazzle and never quit. They eat, breathe, and sleep real estate. I guess for a long time I myself belonged in this category. As has been mentioned elsewhere in this book, I had taken to the habit of writing myself a check from my own account at the beginning of each year and placing it in my wallet. Each year I increased the numbers. A psychological trick. I went from $65,000 to $150,000 to $200,000 to $250,000. Each year I fulfilled the demand I had placed on myself.

©Lynette Yencho

4. *The new hire:* We all know and love this agent—usually young, pretty, and well dressed, full of dreams and hopes of making a fortune in real estate ... and they often do, as you, the reader, also can do. However, if they are not focused and willing to work as is required for any success, some do not survive, as they also were not prepared. They usually go back to other jobs after half a year or one year, at most two years. Sometimes the women simply get married and have a family, a very good choice for some compared to becoming the lonely real estate battle-ax who sits at home alone each night, working the computer at age sixty-five.

5. *The company darling:* These agents are the broker's overall favorite agents. They get all the out-of-town leads and inquiries to follow up on. They also get the corporate

transfer leads and sales. With all my sales over the years and despite the fact that I spoke three languages— English, German, and French—leads were often given to other agents, sometimes to women without any language skills at all. I often did and still do wonder what other services they might have provided. But who knows, and who would tell? Sometimes pet agents can be male, as well, as was the case with my $4 million sale that ended up with giving the pet agent a huge sum he did not earn. But again, who knows and who will tell?

So which one of these could be the right agent for your home sale? After interviewing two or three agents you should be the judge, and the best advice I can give you is to follow your instincts and gut feelings about a person you interviewed. If you like that person, and he or she seems to have energy and enthusiasm, seems honest, and has a track record of good sales, you might want to go with that one. Be wary of the fast-talking agents or the agent without any experience at all. Timid agents will be timid with a buyer too—not a good choice. Loud agents or brash agents may put off a buyer, but you will be the best judge.

Shopping for a buyer's agent

You want to purchase a new home or investment property, but who will you work with? Here are some rules to follow:

1. Don't' call a "listing taker," the superhero agent who has all those flashy listings. He or she is not really interested in driving around with you looking at homes until you finally make up your mind. He or she is already making a lot of money, and driving people around would be way too much work. Remember they like to sit back and let other agents sell their listings. The superhero listing agent is not a good choice.

2. The "new hire" will take the time to drive you around and show you as many houses as you want to see. They are hungry and willing to work. But do they know the ropes? Can they give you really good advice after all? How long have they been in the business? This might work out if they refer you to other knowledgeable specialists, such as experienced mortgage brokers, title agents, and so on. They may also get advice from their brokers if they need it. New hires sometimes work with more experienced agents in a team, and then you have the best of all worlds. The newly hired agent can do the driving and showing, and the more experienced agent can write up the contract and lead you through the escrow paperwork with confidence.

3. An old battle-ax is a pretty good choice, as they know the business and have been around. They may not wear the pretty miniskirt that shows their legs, but they know the ropes. They can give advice, as they know the rules and the neighborhoods. They also know other good people in the business who can help you through the escrow process with confidence.

4. The office darling/pet agent is usually pretty busy and stressed out with many escrows going at the same time. Though never an office pet, I often also had three or four escrows going on simultaneously. There is not that much time to give hour-long advice to new buyers. I tended to refer

©Lynette Yencho

new buyers to other agents; they were too time-consuming, and they usually bought low-priced homes they could afford. Was I spoiled? Of course, I was. So the office darling will also make a choice about whom to work with. If you are buying a higher-priced property, this agent will work with you. If you are buying something very inexpensive and below $100,000, the office darling will think twice about working with you, even in a difficult market. It is a matter of economics, as these agents can make better use of their time with a higher-priced property with another buyer/seller.

5. Be careful with the "area specialist"! Ask why they call themselves "area specialist." Ask to see a list of homes they actually sold in the area you are interested in. Some agents have indeed worked in one particular area for a long time (you need at least two years or more to know an area very well), so they will know which home sold for how much and they have seen the home. It is very important to have viewed the properties that have been sold before the sale. As anyone can print out sales from the area Multiple Listing Service, unless they have seen the property, the list means very little. Differences in homes are huge—square footage, amenities, upgrades, size of lot, landscaping, and other factors all make a difference. Some agents will suddenly decide to become an "area specialist" from one day to another and have no in-depth knowledge at all. They hang up a For Sale sign in front of a property (could be their own home) and add "area specialist." Usually people will like the idea of working with such a person, but be aware and ask the right questions … and better yet, ask for written proof of their expertise.

6. Many agents today profess to be "short sale or foreclosure specialists," particularly in these changed times of fallen

values. There are many transactions now involving short sales or foreclosures. Again, be aware!

In Florida I once actually received an e-mail from a less than honorable "foreclosure specialist." I looked at the e-mail and realized this was a step-by-step plan to lure any buyer into the specialist's office with phony lists of foreclosure sales. This person advised any agent who was up for it to place signs saying Foreclosure Property Lists Available strategically for miles around an open house they were sitting in that day. Once the "buyer" arrived, they were to tell that buyer they had just run out of this list and ask him or her to come to the office in half an hour for a completely detailed list of available foreclosure properties.

Once the buyer arrived back at the office, the agent would make an appointment for another day to show the buyer some of these "available homes." Once in the clutches of this dishonorable person/agent, the buyer would end up being pressured into buying a home, with little hope of escaping. Obviously I did not try the scheme myself. So again, "Caveat emptor!" Buyer beware!

In a short sale or foreclosure, the seller has to complete extensive paperwork, and supply bank statements for many months, hardship letters with periodic updates, copies of listings showing reduced prices of the property, and other documents.

The agent will take the listing and hope that a buyer will show up, represented usually by another agent, the buyer's agent. When a buyer makes an offer to the seller, he or she has to accompany that offer with proof of funds for the purchase and an estimated "HUD-1" or closing statement, which has to be supplied by an attorney who handles closings or a title company. The listing agent will not do any of that.

Again, the agent just takes the listing and hopes to find a buyer as soon as possible to get the commission. Many short sales or foreclosure sales will not close, as the lenders often are not willing to accept the low offered purchase prices. They have made their own appraisal of the value of the property. The lender may counter the offer from the buyer, or they may simply toss the offer into the wastebasket. One never knows.

I would say that an agent who claims to have closed a lot of short sales and is an expert on them must possess infinite patience or must be desperate.

7. "The obsessively working agent" (yes, again) is probably your best choice. This agent will work no matter what. He or she thrives on too much work, on the overload. This agent will drive you around for weeks, even if the chances of your buying anything at all are slim. This agent is motivated by what might be and probably has a lot of bills to pay at home. He or she has lots of energy and will spend it freely on you. This is the agent who also makes cold calls to anyone on a given street anywhere to get a listing and will be grateful to have a buyer to work with.

I mentioned an agent in California before who spent hours on the phone every single day, until he would hit on someone who actually thought about selling a home. That is how he made his living. It was very hard work, but the numbers played out for him. I could never and have never made cold calls, simply could never cope with the ugly rejections people would give him. He was only trying to make a living, but he rarely spoke with a nice person. He had become very thick-skinned and just shook it off; at least he never showed us any hurt feelings. He would get a new listing about once a month in the medium- to high-price range—which meant from $500,000 to $850,000 at the time in California—and sell the house quickly. Thus he was able to meet his own high financial obligations every month.

Of all the real estate agents types above, you will simply have to make a choice and decision, but I hope to have given you some guide lines and insight. After all, a good agent can make all the difference in selling or buying a property. They know where the good neighborhoods are, the marginal ones and the least desirable. They know pricing and have access to all recent sales in a given area for better understanding of the market in that area. That is still the same and always will be. A good agent can save you a lot of money, help avoid bad choices and bad investments, help with making the right choices for you and are worth their weight in gold, but only if they are truly interested in helping you and not just in making their commission. Unfortunately many agents today fall into the last category.

The dual agent

A "dual agent" represents both the buyer and the seller and usually works as a transaction broker. This can happen when an agent takes a listing and a buyer approaches this agent to purchase the home or investment property. In some states this is not allowed and is actually against the law. Other states will permit this dual agency, as long as it is disclosed on all documents and both the buyer and the seller are aware of the situation. An agent can be a dual agent in a special capacity, as in a transaction broker agency. As a single agent, the person has an obligation to represent the buyer or seller with utmost honesty, and to disclose all know facts involving the transaction to his or her client. When one works as a transaction broker, this arrangement changes somewhat. You don't have exclusive fiduciary duty to either party, buyer or seller.

I have represented both buyer and seller in California many times as a transaction broker, and it always has gone smoothly. The key is disclosure by the agent to all parties involved.

A good agent will know how to overcome buyer's or seller's remorse; this agent will make sure that a written and signed contract with all deposits made on time is executed, that inspections within the time frame of the contract are made, and that all contingencies are removed within the allowed days of the contract. All that will keep the buyer and seller on their toes and within the contract. They will thank you later for this efficiency and professionalism.

Both buyer and seller should receive a written timeline (transaction calendar) of their contract with all important dates clearly shown and highlighted, as was previously noted. This is an extremely important part of your job if you want to be a successful Realtor. If you are sloppy about your contracts and don't pay attention to the deadlines, you may find yourself without a sale. No one will help you with this—not your broker or anyone else in your office—unless you ask. The brokers may be too busy to give you advice all the time. However, if you find that your broker may not have time when you have a question, you can ask your fellow agents; most are more than willing to help you out. If you don't ask, you don't get an answer. Again, don't be shy about asking!

CHAPTER 15

Auctions

Obviously auctions don't require an agent. They are handled by the court systems after the property is given for auction by the lender, or by an auction company that specializes in real estate sales. Anyone can hire an auctioneer and try to auction off a property they want to get rid of. Bidding auctions, however, seldom bring the desired results. Sellers are usually unwilling to sell for the low prices people will offer at auctions. The auctioneer will make a commission only if the property sells. If it does not, he or she will go away unpaid. I have attended numerous auctions of this type, and the properties all remained unsold, but that does not always have to be the case. To find auctions in your area check with your county courthouse, and they will provide you with the dates and times. Sometimes they are listed on the Internet, at sites such as i.e. www.jacksoncounty.org. Obviously you have to fill in your own county information.

There are two types of auctions:

At *absolute auctions* the seller has to accept any price received by the auctioneer, and at *regular auctions* the seller can refuse the bid prices and has previously set a reserve price with the auction company. Absolute auctions are rare, but if you can locate a good property being sold through an absolute Auction, if might be worth your time to go and have a look at it. The seller has to accept the offered best price, and you need to make a 10 percent cash or check down payment on the spot, with the balance usually due in thirty days at close of escrow when you receive the title to the property. Since there will be enough time from the sale to close of escrow, you might be able to get financing for the purchase with good credit scores and proof of income.

Lenders will auction off properties they hold through the courts or auctioneers after a property has been foreclosed on. They are willing to accept less money to reduce their vast inventory of homes in foreclosure at this time. If you have cash, you can make a very good buy at an auction. The properties to be auctioned may be listed at the various courthouses in their counties. You will have to invest the time to go to the courthouse, read your newspapers, and explore whether some properties are on the calendar for auction. To purchase at a regular auction you also must bring cash or a sizable down payment and pay the balance in cash within so many days. The www.auction.com site also lists with real estate offices in the neighborhood.

Foreclosures

Banks give listings of foreclosed homes for sale to a real estate brokerage. The property is then drastically reduced in price to attract a buyer.

Since the owners don't live in the home anymore and have not paid the mortgage and taxes for a long time, these homes are usually in great disrepair. They will often require a large amount of cash to get them back up to a livable condition, on the inside and the outside. Therefore it is sometimes questionable if a foreclosure sale is really a good buy, despite the tempting advertisements you may read. Before you invest in a foreclosure sale, make sure you know the average market values of homes in the neighborhood and get some bids on work that the property needs. If you pay more than the market value of the other homes in the area and have to invest more funds into repairs and improvements, you did not make a good deal in purchasing this foreclosure property.

A house in my neighborhood in Florida sold as a foreclosed property through the bank that held the note. The listing was then given to an agent. It sold for far below market value, but it needed a new pool, a new pool enclosure, new floors, new carpets, new kitchen, new paint/wallpaper, and new landscaping. It had become a jungle around the property, with even a sighting of a Florida panther, rats running around, etc. The interior was moldy, the pool was green, bathroom tiles were cracked, and the screens around the pool were torn. There were broken tiles everywhere around the pool and in the bathrooms ... it was a sad sight. The new owners had to invest a huge amount of money to get it up to par again ... maybe not worth all the trouble after all. However, if you are a contractor and can do the

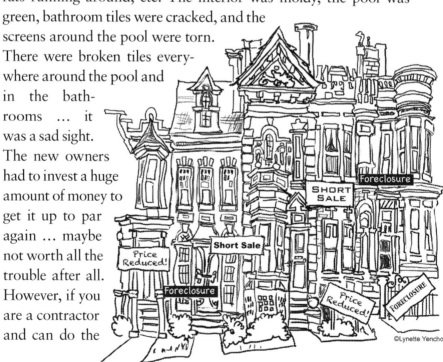

©Lynette Yencho

work yourself and have the time, restoring such a property might be a worthy project.

A property I bid on in the Midwest recently was overpriced by Fannie Mae, so I brought in a lower bid, which was refused by the person handling the foreclosure. I did not go up in my bid, as the property needed too much work—such as a new kitchen, new baths, paint, and carpets—to warrant a higher price. There was no upside potential for a sale with a reasonable profit. I walked away from that property.

One very important thing to keep in mind in any real estate dealing is that there is always another property! Whether you purchase a home or buy as an investor, don't get hung up on one property! There is an unending supply of houses in this country, and there is always another house you might like even better. And never fall in love with a property as an investor; you will get blinded and lose sight of the financial aspects of it, which could cost you dearly.

For information on foreclosures, see www.HomePath.com (Fannie Mae properties), www.HomeSteps.com (Freddie Mac properties), www.RealtyBid.com and more.

Fannie Mae and Freddie Mac are the government entities that underwrite certain loans. They now hold thousands and thousands of homes in foreclosure across the country. To find out more, go to Google and research them; it is all clearly spelled out for you. There is too much information to address here.

Short sales

In a short sale the owner still owns the property; the lender has not foreclosed or taken back the property yet. The owner may be behind in mortgage payments and taxes. In 2008/2009 many homes were sold as a short sale, as values fell below the loan amount people owed their banks. Let us say you bought a house for $385,000 in 2005. You made your 20 percent cash down payment, or $77,000 of your hard-earned money, to purchase and had a $308,000 mortgage to pay for thirty years!

Suddenly, due to no fault of your own, your house is worth only $200,000! That is $108,000 less that you owe the bank! This happened to millions of people during the crash of 2008/2009 ... including me with an investment house I had bought just before the crash.

No one foresaw such a horrible reduction in property values ... not even seasoned agents like me! I had no choice but to place that rental house on the market as a short sale, and I realized a sale for it of only $185,000 six months later. It had been appraised by the bank for $385,000 when I purchased it. I had lost my $77,000 down payment, plus my closing costs, and I lost the house. The bank lost nothing. They had my down payment and my paid bank fees, and they still owned the house until the next sale, when they would receive new fees and interest for years to come.

My credit was impaired after the sale; I had had many sleepless nights and was told that I could not buy again for four years. That was later changed, and the waiting time after a short sale or foreclosure is only one year at the time of this writing. But that may not be the case in some states.

Millions of people suffered such losses due to the money games the large banks are playing on Wall Street. To top it off, the taxpayers (many of whom had lost their homes), bailed them out with their tax dollars! And the big-bank CEOs have continued to rake in millions in bonuses every year since. Think about it!

As a general rule before the crash, real estate values would go through a ten-year cycle; every ten years the values would decline, and then they would go up again to reach another peak ten years later. But 2008/ 2009 was not just a decline; it was a worldwide tsunami created by our good old bankers!

CHAPTER 16

The story about Nathan

I inherited the listing for Nathan's property by accident, a sad one at that. Nathan owned a two-bedroom, two-bath condo in a golfing community in Florida.

I had called the listing agent about a rental for two months in season for a client. Rents in season in Florida bring twice as much income per month to the owners. Consequently many owners rent out their properties during season, which lasts from December through April, a beautiful time there. The temperatures are perfect for golf and polo, swimming and the beach, and it is not humid or too hot.

The listing agent told me that I could not preview the condo, as the owner was a painter/artist and the apartment was in disarray because of all his paintings and materials. I looked at the photos of the condo, which were nice. I bought the story and wrote up a contract for some prospective out-of-town tenants for their rental time, which was six months away.

When I called again to bring the agent the lease and the down payment, he told me that he was in the hospital with a broken femur. I went to visit him and took the documents. The poor person was almost delirious and barely able to handle the paper-work. When I called again some days later to inquire about his health, the hospital told me that he had died. It was quite a shock.

I was now in a position where I had to contact the owner of the condo, so I went to see him after I called. I was in for another shock. The condominium was in a terrible state. The so-called painter had trash piled up on the floors everywhere. The kitchen was filthy, and the bathrooms smelled like a Parisian public toilet.

I did not think I would ever be able to rent this place out. But the owner assured me it would be totally cleaned up for the sea-sonal tenants, and I agreed to move forward with it, against my normal rules. The modern furnishings were very nice and more than adequate, and the location was very nice. I thought that I could always find the prospective tenants something else when they were about to arrive, and my inspection prior to the arrival was not satisfactory. We made an agreement to have the condo professionally cleaned before the clients arrived.

When the time came for the seasonal rental, I went to look at the property and learned to my surprise that the owner would sleep in his car while the place was rented for three months at that high price. He had cleaned it up completely and it sparkled. I realized then that the owner was in desperate need of this rental income to keep his home from going into foreclosure, and I decided to help him all I could. I was able to rent his condo for several seasons from then on; I even brought some of my decor items and went out to buy cutlery, pots and pans, and nice dishes for the seasonal tenants. The arrangement worked out well, but it required a lot of effort on my part. However, to my knowledge the owner still lives in his home and has not lost it. My guess is that the agent who died had also helped this client to squeeze by foreclosure for some time.

A sad deal story

After receiving my monthly flyer about activities such as "sold" and "newly listed" properties in my farm area, I received a call from the owner of a house in a country club area. The house was located on a steep hill, like thousands of houses in California, and it was in the process of being cleaned up by the owner himself after a long rental period to tenants. The client had taken a small apartment in the city, where he lived with his Hispanic wife and her mother. He was middle-aged, about fifty-five years old or so, and in good shape and health.

I agreed to take the listing, and we also agreed on a price after researching comparable sales in the area. I advised him what should be done to make the house sell faster; that is, some painting, yard cleanup, and general maintenance. It was a nice, large home with a few steps leading down from the road into the entrance, the kitchen on that entry level, and the living room one level farther down, with high ceilings and a nice view over trees and the golf course in the distance.

We agreed on a timeline for listing the property on the MLS, and the first open house for agents was scheduled two weeks later to give him time to get the house into shape. Everything was proceeding nicely and as expected. The agents' open house went well; there was a lot of interest in the property, so we planned a public open house shortly thereafter.

The owner was still working on the property and was painting the fence leading to the house when I received a frantic call from his wife, who could barely speak English. I had a hard time understanding her very emotional call. She told me that her husband had suffered a stroke while painting the railing. It was stunning, as he seemed to be in perfect health. I met with her and her husband at the apartment in the city. I did my best to comfort her and told her that the sale of the house was in good hands with me. The husband was able to understand, could speak, and could write with his right hand, but he had difficulty moving his left arm and leg and would be in therapy, of course.

Luckily I received an offer for the house very quickly—a very good one. I took it to the city, and the owner signed the sale documents; I helped them through the process of the sale and the closing. The sale ended well after a bad surprise. The wife now had the funds to take care of her husband's treatment and to live comfortably with him and her mother in their apartment in the city.

Every real estate deal is different from the next one. There is never an easy one or a routine one. You have to be prepared for all events, whether they involve economical, emotional, or health matters, or surprise events.

The out-of-town foreign seller story

As I said before, an agent never experiences the same transaction twice. This is very good for the agent, as it supplies endless experience and novelty, but it can also be difficult at times.

One day I received a referral from an acquaintance who had been born in the Philippines. His aunt of ninety years wanted to sell her large home in Hillsborough, south of San Francisco. I took the listing over the phone and fax, as the old lady was living in the Philippines herself and owned a hospital there, where she was also residing. The home, which she had purchased brand-new, just two years before at age eighty-eight for cash, was built into a hillside, was over four thousand square feet, and was on three levels. It was a stunning home with a four-car garage and all the modern amenities of the time. It also boasted great views over many hills, and she wanted $2.75 million it.

I did not see any problem with the price point; it was a property close to Silicon Valley and within an easy distance to San Francisco. Many houses in the area were purchased by people coming from this fairly new tech area at that time. A lot of money was floating around in Silicon Valley.

I held open houses a couple of times, with only the local residents showing up for information purposes, as is usually the case. Everyone wants to know what goes on in the neighborhood, and that is quite normal. Often you may get a buyer through a neighbor, a relative who wants to move closer to the friend, or a family member. I loved neighbors, as I always could get valuable information from these people.

The client in the Philippines was pleased when I called to tell her that I had a great offer for her. I also had to tell the client that there was a federal law that non–US citizens or foreigners had to pay 10 percent right off the top of the sales price in escrow to the IRS for taxes; this tax was paid by the title company handling the escrow. She did not like to hear it, but she accepted it. Apparently no one had informed her about this "little" taxation problem when she had purchased the home new. I advised her to get a tax attorney and accountant who might be able to help her in regard to the taxes and perhaps obtain a refund.

The escrow closed shortly thereafter, as it was a cash purchase. These cash closings usually can be handled within two weeks or so, as was said before. The title company that closed the sale transferred the funds to the Philippines according to my seller's instructions, minus the 10 percent tax to the IRS. My astute ninety-year old Philippine client negotiated my commission to a much lesser amount, but it was still more than the one I would have received had another buyer's agent been involved. I was happy, the seller was happy—according to several phone calls I received later from her—and I hope that the buyers enjoyed their new home.

CHAPTER 17

Homeownership versus renting—the pros and cons

Lately articles have been written and voices have been heard saying that the American Dream of home ownership is not what it is made out to be and that renting is much more desirable. A tenant does not have to worry about the upkeep of a property and does not have to pay property taxes or insurance; he or she worries only about the monthly rent and therefore has more spending money. Of course, if you want to spend all you make and are content with being a tenant and doing a minimum of work on the place you rent, that would be perfect.

On the other hand, you don't build equity in a rental property; your landlord does, even in these times. Property values are on the rise again, thankfully. Over time your tenants will pay down your loan, and your equity in the property increases every month. As a landlord you can write off the loan payments, property taxes, and insurance payments, plus improvement costs and maintenance costs from your income every year. That is a big plus. You can also depreciate the property (consult with your accountant about this). If you own income properties, Uncle Sam rewards you with tax benefits.

Even as a home owner without income properties, you can deduct the cost of your mortgage interest and your property taxes every year of your ownership. When you sell, you can deduct the improvement costs from your capital gain. The expenses of two homes may be deducted from your income every year! You may have a home you live in most of the time and a vacation home. What an advantage!

As a tenant you have none of these advantages; you receive no tax benefits. Furthermore, you are at the mercy of the landlord and may have to move every year, the worst-case scenario. Who wants to do that? It is tedious, with a lot of work and time wasted.

I believe it is easy to see that home ownership has definite benefits and is a step toward building a future of financial security and wealth, even today—and this will always be so.

In closing, I would like to add that I hope you enjoyed this book and learned both from my knowledge gained over many years and also from my mistakes! You now know the ground rules, and you can always refer back to the book in the future. Thank you for reading it, and go out now and make your millions, whether you are an aspiring agent, home owner, or investor!

EPILOGUE

As a young stewardess in Berlin, Germany, I was working on a flight from Berlin to Frankfurt one day. To my surprise an older gypsy woman came onboard in the morning and sat down in an aisle seat. I had never seen a gypsy in her colorful clothes on a flight before. While I was walking past her during the flight, she took my hand and asked if she could read my palm. I was intrigued, as I also had never had my palm read. She looked at it for a while and then said, "You will be crossing the ocean soon, and you will always be in furs and pearls." I was stunned, as I had not even contemplated leaving Berlin at that time; Berlin was my home. But I did leave after a year, and yes, the gypsy woman had been right; I did become successful in America through hard work and with much drive of my own to succeed. And so can you, if you decide to go for it!

INDEX

ABOUT THE AUTHOR

Barbara Knauf was born in Germany and is a successful real estate investor with twenty years of experience in the industry. She worked as a Realtor in both California and Florida. She has bought and sold many properties for herself and hundreds of clients. She now lives in Kansas City, Missouri, and has two daughters and four grandchildren. Barbara is also a painter/artist; Her websites are www.barbara-anna-knauf.artistwebsites.com or www.artfinder.com/barbara-knauf.

She has written three children's books and a book of poetry, available on www.amazon.com. Go to the website and type Barbara Knauf into the search bar in the book section to view her books.

www.realestatefortunesbarbaraknauf.com